Dear Reader:

The book you are about to read is the latest bestseller from the St. Martin's True Crime Library, the imprint the *New York Times* calls "the leader in true crime!" Each month, we offer you a fascinating account of the latest, most sensational crime that has captured the national attention. St. Martin's is the publisher of perennial bestselling true crime author Jack Olsen whose SALT OF THE EARTH is the true story of one woman's triumph over life-shattering violence; Joseph Wambaugh called it "powerful and absorbing." Fannie Weinstein and Melinda Wilson tell the story of a beautiful honors student who was lured into the dark world of sex for hire in THE COED CALL GIRL MURDER. St. Martin's is also proud to publish critically acclaimed author Carlton Stowers, whose 1999 Edgar Award-winning TO THE LAST BREATH recounts a two-year-old girl's mysterious death, and the dogged investigation that led loved ones to the most unlikely murderer: her own father. In the book you now hold, DEATH IN TEXAS, veteran reporter and bestselling author Carlton Smith exposes the tragic case of Doris Angleton, a loving mother, brutally murdered.

St. Martin's True Crime Library gives you the stories *behind* the headlines. Our authors take you right to the scene of the crime and into the minds of the most notorious murderers to show you what really makes them tick. St. Martin's True Crime Library paperbacks are better than the most terrifying thriller, because it's all true! The next time you want a crackling good read, make sure it's got the St. Martin's True Crime Library logo on the spine—you'll be up all night!

Charles E. Spicer, Jr.
Senior Editor, St. Martin's True Crime Library

"Well, my obvious question [is]," Wright said, "first off, do you have any idea who might have done this?"

There was an extended silence as Bob considered this.

"I have a few ideas," Bob said finally. "Would you turn the tape off now?"

Wright turned off the tape recorder.

I work for the Houston Police Department, Bob told Wright.

And at that point, Bob told Wright some more things that both bemused and perplexed the detective, and made him realize that there would be nothing about this case that would ever be routine. . . .

DEATH IN TEXAS

CARLTON SMITH

St. Martin's Paperbacks

DEATH IN TEXAS

Copyright © 1999 by Carlton Smith.

ISBN: 0-312-97075-7

Printed in the United States of America

St. Martin's Paperbacks edition/July 1999

St. Martin's Paperbacks are published by St. Martin's Press, 175 Fifth Avenue, New York, N.Y. 10010.

10 9 8 7 6 5 4 3 2 1

ACKNOWLEDGMENTS

The author wishes to thank the many people in Houston who assisted in the preparation of this book. A murder trial can be a wrenching event, and never more so for those with emotional stakes in the outcome. Especially appreciated are: Ted Wilson and Lyn McClellan of the Harris County District Attorney's Office, for sharing their theories of the case and their legal strategies, as well as their post-trial remorse and regrets; Sgt. David Ferguson of the Houston Police Department, for reconstructing the events of his department's investigation; Houston attorneys George Tyson, Stan Schneider and Mark Bennett, for sharing their insights on trial strategy; the *Houston Chronicle*'s Steve Brewer, for the same; Vanessa Leggett, for a unique perspective on Roger Angleton; and Official Court Reporter Judith Fox for her invaluable assistance in locating trial exhibits and preparing transcripts on short notice. Special thanks is due to Skip Hollandsworth of *Texas Monthly*, who generously provided the background of his own look at the Angleton case, *The Bookmaker's Wife*, published in *Texas Monthly* in November, 1997.

ELLA LEE LANE

APRIL 16, 1997

ONE

In the earliest part of the evening, when the shadows were just beginning to creep out from under the oaks and the heat was finally starting to fade, the killer made his move.

He made his way along the side of the house to the door he knew was there; he'd been there before. There had been talk about taping and breaking a window to make it look like a burglary, but for some reason, the killer did not do this. Instead, he glanced at the alarm system's control box. As he expected, it was beeping. A word flashed up at him in the fading light.

"Disarm," it read, and he punched in the code he had memorized, 00032. The beeping stopped, and he settled down to wait, but not before resetting the alarm system. Now, he knew, he was trapped; if he moved, it would set off one of the motion detectors, and if that happened, he would be dead meat. The way it was, all he had to do was remain quiet, unmoving, in the small room off the kitchen, and wait for the target to come to him.

It would not, he knew, be for long. He checked his weapons: two .22-caliber semi-automatic pistols, one with a red-dot-projecting laser sight. As he'd told the client, it was foolproof: "One hundred percent accurate: Where the light goes, so does the bullet," he'd said, and the client was impressed.

It was, perhaps, half an hour later when he heard the first sounds.

A faint beeping came from the front of the house. Beep. Beep. The beeps followed, one after the other. The killer held his breath. Would the beeps stop? Would the target come on ahead? Would she go upstairs, as the client had speculated? Or—if he'd done something wrong, would the target get suspicious and back out of the house?

In that case, should he follow her out and eliminate her outside, in front of the house, in full view of whoever was passing by? There was nothing to do but wait, to see what happened.

The beeps stopped.

She's disarmed, he thought. *Now what? Will she go upstairs? Will she come this way?* Somehow, he knew she would.

The killer waited, frozen in silence. He heard the target approach his position, moving toward the sliding doors on the other side of the narrow corridor from his position. The timing had to be perfect.

Too soon, and she would run, maybe get away. Too late, and she would be outside, in the backyard, where the risks for him would be even greater. The killer heard the sounds of her footsteps. In a quick move, surprising for one with his infirmities, the killer mounted the three stairs from his hiding place and thrust open the door into the hallway.

He saw her with her hand on the sliding door, and in one step, crossed to her side and fired his first shot into her left side about six inches below her armpit, and then another. The muzzle was close enough to scorch the cloth of her blouse.

The target was spun around by the blasts. She looked at him, hardly believing what she was seeing. She didn't go down, as he thought she would. She was strong, he remembered, and athletic. Instead, she began to run—back toward the kitchen, toward escape. The killer fired again, and again, and yet again.

Ten or twelve feet away the target went down in a heap, lying on her side in the transition area between the kitchen and the narrow hall, where the killer had first ambushed her. She lay struggling to get up, to move, to get away. The killer followed after her, changing his weapon.

The target cast her eyes up toward him. There was no doubt she recognized him.

Here was a sight few had ever seen: The tale was in her eyes. They spoke of someone who knew what was happening, but who could not believe it—the look of someone who had been abruptly cast through the barrier of the fantastically impossible into the realm of horrifying reality: This man she knew, this man she had once accepted into her life—this same man was now trying to kill her.

However bizarre the idea, however hard it was to conceive of, it was *really happening to her*.

The killer stood over the target with his second pistol. He pointed the muzzle at her left temple and fired, the shell casing pinging away into the darkness of the kitchen. He moved the barrel an inch or so and fired again, then again, again, and again.

As he watched, the last embers of life left the target, and the killer knew she was dead. He fired twice more to make sure.

Doris McGown Beck Angleton, 46, socialite, millionairess, outlaw, once a so-called trophy wife, mother of twelve-year-old twins, was dead.

It was April 16, 1997, and the exclusive enclave of Houston's River Oaks, the well-appointed home of ex-presidents, ex-astronauts, top money managers, big oil buccaneers, wealthy insurance magnates, and at least one major-league bookmaker, would have something to talk about for years to come.

TWO

It wasn't long after the game had started that Robert Angleton's two girls began to pester him with questions.

"Where's Mom?" Ali and Niki asked, and Angleton shrugged. He told his twins that he thought their mother, his wife, Doris, would be along shortly.

But after a few innings and no Doris, Bob Angleton began calling her on his cell phone, and after that, her pager.

Bob Angleton was The Scream's head coach—the manager, as he referred to himself. The teenage girls' fast-pitch softball team had taken increasing amounts of his time over the previous two years. Both Ali and Niki Angleton were members, as they were of another team, as well. The Angleton twins had become interested in softball a few years before, and Bob meant to give them all the support he could muster, right down to a private batting cage in the backyard.

Later, some of the other parents at the game that night recalled that Bob had seemed a bit more animated than usual, somewhat keyed up.

Bob had always been verbal, but on this night he seemed more demonstrative, at one point even getting into an argument with one of the umpires. At length, however, the game was over, and Bob began collecting the bats, balls, and other equipment. Doris had still not arrived, and as Bob packed the equipment and the girls into his Blazer, the twins wondered again what had become of their mother.

Well, Bob told his daughters, You know Mom . . . sometimes she gets distracted. But Bob could see that Ali and Niki were perplexed by Doris' failure to return to the game, and a little worried.

A little after 9:30 that night, Bob and the girls turned into Ella Lee Lane, a quiet, affluent street just on the edge of the well-heeled River Oaks district of Houston.

As Bob turned the Blazer into the driveway, he saw Doris' Suburban parked in its usual place on the circle drive near the front door. Bob entered the code to open the gate, and drove the Blazer in toward the carport near the rear of the house. It was then that he saw that the rear side-door of the house was open.

Bob backed the Blazer out, back beyond the gate. As he described it later, if the door was open and the dog wasn't out, that probably meant trouble.

Bob dialed 911 on his cellular phone.

"Houston 911, do you need police, fire, or ambulance?" the operator asked.

"I don't know what I need, Operator," Bob said. "I'm at my house, my wife doesn't answer the phone, the back door's ajar, I have children in the car."

"Okay, what city?" the operator asked.

"I'm in Houston."

"Okay, we'll ask the police," the operator said. There was a sound of dialing as the 911 operator transferred the call to the dispatchers of the Houston Police Department.

"I'm going to transfer to the police, sir."

A few seconds later, a police dispatcher came on the line and asked what the problem was. Bob said he didn't *know* what the problem was, only that he hadn't been able to contact Doris and the back door to his house was open.

"I've got my kids with me," Bob told the dispatcher.

Okay, the dispatcher said, police units are on the way.

"Should I go in?" Bob asked.

The dispatcher was willing.

Okay, she said, but keep the phone to your ear.

Niki and Ali began clamoring for Bob to stay in the car and wait for the police. Bob told the dispatcher again that the children were in the car, and that they were saying he should stay put.

Well, the dispatcher said, if you go in, keep the phone on.

"I have to change the batteries," Bob said. The connection was terminated.

Some blocks away from the Angleton house, Houston Police Department Officer K. P. Carr had been monitoring the exchange between the worried homeowner and dispatch.

As Carr later recounted, the word "ajar" sort of leaped out at him across the airwaves.

Ajar? Carr thought. *Who uses the word "ajar" when their house is maybe being burgled?* It just didn't sound right to Carr's cop's ear. He drove over to Ella Lee Lane, arriving perhaps a minute before the patrol officer assigned by dispatch reached the scene.

Carr saw two men standing near the Blazer on the driveway at the front of the house. One was Bob, the other was Bob's friend and business associate, Texas Welsh. There were two girls in the Blazer.

Carr approached the two men and identified himself. He discovered that Bob had not yet entered the house. Bob explained again about the children not wanting him to go inside. Carr moved down the driveway with his flashlight. The side door near the rear of the house appeared to be open a little more than a foot. Carr went inside.

Carr mounted the steps to the interior door, flashing his light ahead of him. On the landing, Carr's foot dislodged something on the ground. He recognized the noise it made as it rolled away. It was a cartridge shell. Carr flashed the light around the interior. A little more than eleven feet away, Carr saw the sprawled body of a woman lying in a pool of blood. From the way she lay motionless, it appeared that she was dead.

Carr made sure, then carefully backed out of the house and retraced his steps down the driveway to the front of the house.

Carr asked Bob what Doris had been wearing, and when Bob told him, Carr indicated that Doris was dead. Bob appeared to get angry, Carr said later, and challenged his expertise in detecting death. When Carr said he could tell Doris was dead, all right, Bob collapsed against him. Carr struggled to hold Bob up. He told him to get a grip on himself, that his daughters were watching. At some point, Bob asked Carr to tell the girls that their mother was dead, but Carr declined to do this.

After Tex Welsh identified himself, arrangements were made for him to take the girls to his house nearby. Meanwhile, Carr called the police department's homicide unit.

Shortly after ten that night, two Houston Police Department homicide detectives arrived at the house.

One was Brian Foster, whose job it would be to take control of the crime scene; the other was Mike Wright, who would have responsibility for interviewing witnesses—namely, Bob, now that the girls had gone to Tex Welsh's house.

Both Foster and Wright took a quick tour of the murder scene. They noted that a number of spent shell casings littered the kitchen and hallway. The rest of the house did not appear to have been disturbed. They noted the condition of the burglar alarm, which was off.

Now Foster wanted Bob's permission to thoroughly search the house, but Bob wouldn't give it, the detectives said later. Bob then called his attorney, George Tyson of Houston, and asked whether he should permit the police to conduct their search.

Absolutely, Tyson told him; so the search began.

As Foster and the crime scene technicians began their work, Wright approached Bob and began to gently question him.

Wright taped the interview.

"I'm Mike Wright of the Houston Police Department Homicide Division, in reference to case number 048356997," Wright said into his recorder.

"And I'm with Robert Angleton. With reference to a possible murder, at 3031 Ella Lee.

"Robert, can you go ahead and tell me what you know of this incident right now, or what happened this evening?"

"Uh, I don't know what happened," Bob said.

"OK. Uh, the events leading up to you coming home and finding the body?"

" 'Kay," Robert said. He took a breath. What was to follow was spoken in a calm, nearly emotionless, truncated monotone, almost as if Bob were describing a routine maintenance job on his car in complete, succinct detail.

"At 6:45, roughly, I left the house headed for the—I'm the head coach, manager of a girls' fast-pitch team over in West U[niversity]. My daughters play on that team. I left the house headed for, we had a game scheduled at 7:45, my wife was to follow up with the children about twenty minutes later.

"Uh, I got to the field, we took some batting practice, my wife pulls up, uh, on the street, at the batting cage, gets out, says she's coming back home, to change, and she'll be back at the game, and I say, when you come back, pick up Ali's bat, she needs it, we're the home team, so—

"Anyway," Bob continued, "so she goes back, we play the game, we're playing out there, and then she hasn't returned, she's not in the stands, so I call. And I beep.

"And . . . it's not unusual for her not to wear a beeper. Well, I didn't get a response. And she didn't call me back on her cell phone. I beeped her again. Called here. And got the machine. Then I got concerned."

"[Was that] out of the ordinary?" Wright asked.

"Yes, it's out of the ordinary, but—kids ask where's Mom, game's over, heading home—"

"About what time was this?"

"Game was over . . . nine . . . twenty-five. Somewhere around there, twenty or twenty-five. Head home as quick as I can, uh . . ."

Wright asked how long this took, but Bob wasn't able to say exactly.

"Anyway," Bob continued, "and [we] pulled into the driveway, headed straight here, make my stop in the driveway, as I always do, hit the button on the gate, opened the gate, pulled in the driveway, back over here. Uh, door's open this much."

Bob indicated the size of the opening with his hands.

"The side door?" Wright asked.

"The side door," Bob agreed. "The door down over there. Open that much. I stop halfway into the driveway. I mean, we're concerned about Mom, uhm, on the way back, why didn't Mom come back to the game?

"And I said, Well, you know Mom, sometimes she . . . anyway, so my first reaction is, Okay, door's open, dog's not out, dog should be out, if the door's open, the dog's [not] out, there's a problem. I back out the driveway and call 911.

"And then I called 911 from the car with the kids, and tell them the situation, they say stay in the car . . . well, I think one of them, I said, Can I get out of the car, and my kids go, No, don't get out of the car, so I sit, stay in the car, and then I call my friend here, who's got the kids right now, he comes over, then I get out of the car, we're standing outside the car, then the officer shows up."

"Okay," Wright said. "When you first got here, Robert, and you drove up and saw the door ajar, what was your first impression? I mean, your wife obviously didn't come back to the game. Did you think it was burglary or something, or something a little more serious, or what?"

"To be honest with you, I called one of her friends—I thought she might be out with a friend having a drink. 'Kay, I called her friend and said, Have you seen Doris? Because this is a friend that she does have drinks with on a reasonably regular

basis. I called her while we were waiting on the police, to see if she'd seen Doris. She said no. So, what
was going through my mind? I mean, I have the kids
starting to cry, and my one daughter is in the back
seat just bawling her head off, so—''

"How old are your daughters?''

"Twelve-year-old twins.''

"Twelve years old.'' Wright nodded.

"So I don't know what I was thinking, really,''
Bob went on. "I was thinking that I have kids with
me right now, the smart thing to do is not rush into
the house.''

Wright nodded.

Bob and Wright talked a bit more about the softball team. Finally, Wright turned the discussion back
to the subject.

"Well, my obvious question [is],'' Wright said,
"first off, do you have any idea who might have done
this?''

There was an extended silence as Bob considered
this.

"I have a few ideas,'' Bob said finally. "Would
you turn the tape off now?''

Wright turned off the tape recorder.

I work for the Houston Police Department, Bob
told Wright.

And at that point, Bob told Wright some more
things that both bemused and perplexed the detective,
and made him realize that there would be nothing
about this case that would ever be routine.

THREE

Later that night—around two in the morning, as Steve McGown recalled it—the telephone rang in Steve's house in North Carolina.

Steve could tell right away from his mother Ann's voice that something bad had happened, and since his father, Randy McGown, had already been through two heart bypass surgeries, he feared the worst.

"I knew from her tone," Steve said later, "somebody had died."

God, he thought, *Daddy died.*

But it wasn't about Randy. It was Doris.

Doris was dead, Ann McGown Borochov told her son. She'd been shot to death in her own house in Houston. She'd heard this from Bob, Ann told Steve; apart from what Bob had told her, she knew nothing.

Steve hung up the telephone; his mind reeled. The idea that someone had shot his big sister to death was at first beyond comprehension.

Why? he thought. Doris McGown had never harmed a living soul. Why Doris? *Shot* to death?

It was absurd. No, it was unthinkable.

Who would do such a thing? Some part of his brain kept insisting that it must be some grotesque mistake, that it hadn't really happened, that he was only dreaming this. But every time he tried to will himself into believing it, the sound of his mother's voice came back to him.

It's Doris . . .

FOUR

Shortly before 7:30 the same morning, even as Steve McGown was flying into Houston from North Carolina, Houston lawyer Thomas R. Conner was glancing through the newspaper; his wife was idly watching the morning news on television. Suddenly, Conner's wife called out to him.

"Did you hear that?" she said. "A woman was murdered in River Oaks last night."

Later, Conner would recall being mildly surprised at this; after all, River Oaks was hardly the sort of neighborhood where murder was to be expected, unlike other districts of the sprawling environs of the nation's fourth-largest city.

It wasn't that people in River Oaks were immune to human passions, it was just that they were more likely to settle their disputes with writs rather than revolvers. Like, for instance, one of his most recent clients, Doris McGown Angleton.

Doris had first contacted Conner, one of Houston's leading matrimonial lawyers, in December. She wanted a divorce from her husband of almost fifteen years, Robert Nicholas Angleton; and then Doris had proceeded to explain to Conner exactly why she wanted to split up from Bob, and what she wanted done to protect her interests.

As an experienced divorce lawyer, Conner had grown accustomed to seeing many different demeanors from his varied clients, many of whom were well-to-do. Some cried much of the time, or evinced seething anger. But there was little of either emotion in Doris Angleton.

"Well, it's just that Doris was not an emotional client," Conner said later.

"Many women, understandably, when they're going through something like this, and some men, for that matter, are very emotional, they're high-strung about it, they tend to have episodes when they're weepy, and Doris was just not that kind of person. She was very collected and very cool."

To Conner, Doris confided what had long been an open secret among a select circle of River Oaks' high-toned social set: her husband, Bob, was an outlaw—an illegal bookmaker, and one with some very special connections inside the Houston Police Department.

Oh sure, Bob had a legitimate business, a courier service called Roadrunner Couriers, Inc., as well as real-estate holdings and several other investments.

But the real money, Doris told Conner, was in the commissions Bob and his associates charged bettors anxious to wager on college and professional football and basketball.

These commissions, ten percent of each amount bet, had grown into millions over the years as Bob's book had prospered while other bookmakers' take had declined.

How had that happened? It was because in addition to being an illegal bookmaker, Bob had an auxiliary role: He was also the Houston Police Department's primary informant on bookmaking.

In effect, Bob was ratting out his competitors, with the complete knowledge and cooperation of the police who were supposed to be enforcing the law against everyone.

As Bob's book prospered from the 1980s into the 1990s, Doris told Conner, the take had grown to staggering proportions: millions in cash, much of it stashed in various safe-deposit boxes in sundry banks around town.

But now Doris wanted out. She especially wanted two things: a freeze on Bob's safe-deposit boxes, to prevent him from running off with the communal assets, however illegally obtained; and second, a way back into the straight world.

That meant, somehow, making Doris' share of the illegal cash legitimate. Otherwise, the Internal Revenue Service might claim anything Doris might net from the divorce as back taxes, penalties, and interest.

Indeed, Doris herself might face criminal sanctions, to say nothing of Bob.

After considering Doris' situation, Conner had come to a decision: He referred Doris to a prominent Houston tax lawyer. Doris met with the tax lawyer on Thursday, April 10; and while the specifics of the lawyer's advice to Doris would never be disclosed, it seems highly likely that Doris was told that the only way back into the straight world was to file an amended joint tax return—*with Bob*.

In the meantime, Conner had drafted a court order freezing a number of safe-deposit boxes that Doris knew about; the order prevented Bob or anyone else from opening those boxes.

FIVE

While the Angleton divorce was unusual in some ways—Conner was later to say it was the first time he'd ever asked a divorce court to freeze multiple bank safe-deposit boxes—it was just another new wrinkle in terms of Conner's normal clientele.

Conner, in fact, was well-known in the River Oaks community, having represented a number of other wealthy and socially prominent clients; Doris had been referred to him by Tommy and Julie Hughes, who were among the beneficiaries of the Howard Hughes fortune. Tommy and Julie were good friends of both Doris's and Conner's, so it was natural that Conner would come to represent Doris when she wanted a divorce.

The Angletons and the Hugheses were among a smart set of relatively young movers and shakers in the River Oaks area, often upwardly mobile couples well-connected to the banking, oil and gas, insurance, real estate, and other business interests that were transforming Houston.

The oil boom of the 1970s and the early 1980s metamorphosed the city into a modern megalopolis of gigantic, air-conditioned, steel and glass stelae that sprouted with surprising suddenness in Houston's downtown core, cheek by jowl with older, smaller buildings from the 1940s and 1950s, which themselves were encrustations atop the remnants of Spanish and Creole architecture left over from an earlier century. It was all a long way from the quieter years before the go-go boom that lit up the Texas oil industry in the 1970s.

From the heights attained on the top floors of the new Houston, one could see a nearly flat landscape rolling off into the impenetrable distance, a vast wooded plain slightly cut by the meandering, west-to-east course of Buffalo Bayou, a natural drainage swale that emptied into Galveston Bay just east of the city.

Houston is a metropolis built for the automobile, vast in its expanse, nearly 600 square miles in area, three times that amount for the whole of Harris County. Its downtown core is ringed and streamed by a series of freeways designed to move the county's three million people from suburb to central city and back again with a minimum of disruption.

If one had a downtown office window facing the right direction, one could see the timbered enclave of River Oaks, and the privileged precincts of the River Oaks Country Club, south of Interstate 10 and Houston's Memorial Park, just east of Interstate 610, the ring freeway that ties the city together. Interstate 10 bisects the city and county; go far enough to the west and one reaches the heart and soul of Texas, San Antonio, and the Alamo; to the east one emerges into the Cajun rhythms of Baton Rouge and New Orleans. Interstate 45 connects the city to the warm sea currents of the Gulf at Galveston, and to the higher and dryer cattle and cotton country in the north at Dallas.

By the nineties, much of Houston's growth had spread to the west side of the city, south of I-10 and east of I-610, the so-called West Loop, where a new crop of steel-and-glass towers began to emerge. One of the world's largest and most exclusive indoor shopping districts, the Galleria, became a magnet for such pricey retail establishments as Marks and Spencer, Lord & Taylor, Saks, Neiman Marcus and other high-end emporiums. Surrounding the shopping mecca were acres of fresh-cut green lawns adorning high-rise office towers, places where mega-deals were cut, enormous profits suddenly realized, and the good life was waiting at home around an inviting swimming pool, an expansive patio, all surrounded by estate-sized lots, populated by neighbors on the same stratospheric trajectory of success, such as Bob and Doris Angleton.

Perhaps because the vast bulk of its growth took place only over the past fifty years—the city of Houston alone grew from a bit less than 600,000 in 1950 to 1.6 million in 1990—there has always been a bit less respect for old traditions in Houston than in some other areas of Texas. When he thought about the differences between Houston and other parts of Texas, Conner was aware of a difference in tone, or attitude, between the state's two largest cities.

"Well, Houston's much more wide open than Dallas," Conner later observed. By that, Conner meant that Houston is a bit edgier than Dallas; Houston is the sort of environment where risk was always an element of the equation, and where people often have an eye out for the main chance, unlike Dallas-Fort

Worth, where who you are depends as much on who your daddy was as what you do.

"Dallas tends to think they're better than the rest of the state, and Houston's more of a wide-open, friendlier city," Conner explained. In other words, Houston is to be a place where people tend to accept others at face value; and if someone was rumored to be skirting close to the edge of the law, there was more room for nudges and winks; after all, the attitude seemed to be, if there was no harm, there was no foul.

Asked if Houston tended to be more new money, while Dallas might be seen as more old money, Conner agreed.

"That's probably a somewhat fair comparison," Conner said. "I think both cities have their share of nouveau riche, and I think Dallas, the old guard in Dallas, may have managed to keep the gates closed longer than the old guard in Houston has been able to. Because in the society columns in Houston, now you see more and more names that are really from the new rich, that they don't have the family backgrounds and connections that would have been required, say, twenty-five years ago."

Still, that morning when he thought of Dallas-Fort Worth as he drove to his office in downtown Houston, Conner was reminded of an old case he'd once handled there—especially in the light of the morning's news about a woman having been murdered in a place like River Oaks.

The Fort Worth matter had been a divorce case. Conner was one of several attorneys who represented a woman named Priscilla Davis, who was married to a man reputed to be one of the richest men in Texas, Cullen Davis. In the late 1970s, Priscilla Davis, her boyfriend, and her daughter were shot to death in Fort Worth. Cullen Davis had been charged with the crimes but was found not guilty. Later, Davis had been charged with plotting to kill the judge in the divorce case, and had been found not guilty of that, as well. *That* had been a strange case, Conner thought, one for a lifetime.

Conner had nearly put the Davis case out of his mind, along with the River Oaks murder, when he entered his office. His bookkeeper sought him out.

"Have you heard the news?" she asked. "Doris Angleton was murdered last night."

SIX

At once Conner's mind flashed back to the Priscilla Davis murder. As Conner was later to admit, the next thing that went through his mind was the question of whether Doris' estranged husband, Bob, might be involved.

"It's the first thing that goes through your mind, correctly or incorrectly," Conner said. "There's a divorce going on, and one of the parties is murdered."

That was the thinking of the Houston area news media, as well. Within a matter of hours after learning of Doris Angleton's death, reporters from radio, television, and the newspapers had checked the courthouse for information on Doris Angleton, and had learned that she was seeking a divorce from Bob Angleton—along with the rather unusual information about the sealing of the safe-deposit boxes. Naturally, one of the first people the reporters called was Conner. The reporters wanted to know whether Conner thought Bob was responsible for the murder.

Conner wasn't about to touch that one—especially not after the Cullen Davis case. I've got no comment, Conner told the reporters. No comment.

At just about the same time that Conner was learning about the murder of Doris Angleton, the body of his client was reposing on a stainless-steel table at the offices of the Harris County Medical Examiner, just a short distance from the Astrodome in downtown Houston.

Doris, Assistant Medical Examiner Dr. Tommy J. Brown noted, had been five feet five inches tall, and had weighed 123 pounds when she died. The reasons for her death were perfectly obvious to Brown: Doris had been shot to pieces, most notably by seven separate gunshot wounds along the left side of the head.

There were other wounds as well: One bullet had entered Doris' left side about seven inches below the top of her shoulder, went through the left lung, through the heart, through the right lung, out of her body, and then into her right arm, where it finally stopped. Dr. Brown removed it.

A second wound in the same area also sliced through both lungs and wound up in the upper right arm. Brown recovered that one, too.

There was another wound in the upper left abdomen. This one severed the left renal artery and fractured Doris' lower spine.

There was a wound in the right buttock, in which the bullet track angled slightly downward, which suggested that the shooter might have been somewhat taller than Doris, and firing at her as she moved away. The wound was through-and-through, so Brown could not recover the bullet.

There were two other wounds, as well, also through-and-through: one in Doris' left forearm, the other in the back of Doris' left upper arm. Both of these wounds seemed to indicate that Doris had had her back to the shooter.

It appeared that the brunt of the attack had come on Doris' left, rear side; that she had been hit, had tried to move away from the shooter, and had fallen to the floor. The major anomaly was the entrance wound in the abdomen; if all the other wounds were from the left rear, what did a wound from the front mean?

Brown looked at the head wounds next. Beginning a little more than four inches down from the top of the head, in Doris' left temple area, a series of wounds marched back toward the rear of Doris' skull in fairly precise order—seven different precisely defined holes. Curiously, Brown noted no soot or stippling—from burned gunpowder residue—around the area of any of these wounds.

Had the open muzzle of the gun been within inches of Doris' head, such burning or stippling was to be expected. However, the pattern of the wounds—so close together—seemed to rule out the possibility that the wounds had been inflicted from a significantly longer distance; in that case, the shooter would have to be an almost inhumanly accurate marksman, especially if Doris was still alive when the head wounds occurred, as seemed obvious by the amount of bleeding in Doris' brain.

There wasn't a gun-handler alive who could put such a tight pattern of shots into one side of Doris' head, especially if a wounded Doris was weaving and bobbing as she tried to get away. The most logical explanation for the lack of soot and stippling was that the shooter had covered Doris' head with something, perhaps a cloth or a pillow, as he or she fired the fatal shots, while Doris lay dying from the lung, spine, and heart shots.

Brown put Doris' head onto the usual ceramic block, jaw forward, left side of the head exposed to the camera; a photograph was taken of the seven head entrance wounds, small round holes in the skull, now shaven by a technician; marching one after the other to the rear of the brain, they were the tracks of small particles of lead that had stolen the life, future, and soul of Doris McGown Angleton.

Brown eventually recovered nine bullets and fragments of bullets from Doris' body, all of them small caliber, all appearing to be .22s. Which in turn suggested one more thing: Doris Angleton had hardly surprised a burglar. Whoever shot Doris Angleton had meant to make sure she was dead.

SEVEN

All the way to Houston, on the flight he'd hurriedly arranged, Steve McGown kept thinking of his sister.

Why, Doris? Why would someone shoot you? Tell me what happened.

"I guess by the time I landed," Steve said later, "there were two things that I felt certain of: Number one, where in the house she'd been killed, and two, I knew that she knew who killed her."

Steve rented a car. He wasn't that familiar with Houston, and wasn't sure how to get to the Angleton house. Nor did he know his brother-in-law, Bob, all that well, because whenever he visited Doris, Bob was usually working.

Doris, just get me there, Steve thought, and somehow without making a single wrong turn, he found his way to Ella Lee Lane.

Steve pulled up in front. There was a man in a suit talking on a cellular telephone. Another man with a television camera stood nearby. Steve looked at the house. Inside, he could see people moving around.

Steve went up to the man with the camera.

"Are the police here?" he asked.

No, he was told, they've gone.

Steve wasn't sure what to do. After hesitating a bit, he went to the front door and knocked. A man he didn't know answered.

"Can I help you?" Tex Welsh asked.

"I'm Steve. Doris' brother."

Tex nodded. "Yeah," he said. "You look like her." Tex opened the door and let Steve in.

Tex told Steve that Bob and the girls were over at his house. Tex and another man were cleaning up the blood on the kitchen floor and patching the bullet holes in the walls.

"Tell me one thing," Steve said. "Where was she killed?"

Before Tex could give him an answer, Steve provided one.

"She was going to the loft, wasn't she?" Steve asked.

Tex looked startled. "How did you know?" he asked.

"I guess she told me," Steve said.

Later, after Tex and the other man left, Steve sat down alone in the living room, thinking about his sister.

She'd been going to the loft, Steve thought. Upstairs, over the game room. Where the computers were. Where Doris had been going on-line. Where Doris had met some new people who were about as different from Bob Angleton as you could get. Doris had been killed while she was on her way to visit with her new friends.

Steve counted the bullet holes in the walls. He found five. Tex had told him that Doris had been shot thirteen times.

"I knew no pistol held thirteen bullets," he said later. "So I knew the person who'd done this had to reload. There was nothing disturbed in the house. There was nobody there to rob. Nobody was there to do anything but kill my sister. That was the only reason for it—just for murder.''

EIGHT

That was pretty much the same conclusion that the Houston Police Department's homicide division had already reached on the same morning, after reviewing the events of the night before.

By this time, Detectives Foster and Wright were off. Normally, the pair who had caught the case would stay with it, returning to it when they came back on duty. But because of the high profile of a River Oaks murder, it was decided higher up the chain of command to shift another pair of detectives over to the follow-up so the investigation could continue without interruption.

Thus, two Houston Police Department plainclothes sergeants, David Ferguson and Jerry Novak, were temporarily detailed to carry the case forward.

Ferguson and Novak were normally the senior partners with their own two-person teams. But since each of their partners happened to be off that day, Nelson Zoch, the lieutenant in charge, put Ferguson and Novak together that morning to work on the follow-up.

What was clear to both Ferguson and Novak was that the killing of Doris Angleton was almost certainly a planned event.

Fact One: The Angleton house showed no signs of burglary. The burglar alarm had not been tripped, there were no signs of forced entry. There was no disarray inside the house, no evidence of frantically searched drawers or pried-open cabinets. Officers at the scene had noticed an open safe, and called it to Bob's attention. But Bob, according to the officers who talked to him, told them that the safe was always kept open, and there was nothing of value in it.

Fact Two: What sort of burglar shoots someone thirteen times? Once, maybe, or twice, but then it's time to beat feet. That Doris Angleton was shot over a dozen times almost certainly meant that she had been targeted for murder by someone who came prepared to do exactly that. Further, the presence of so many wounds seemed to suggest that the shooter either had two guns or had paused to reload. What sort of burglar would do that?

Fact Three: Because the alarm didn't go off when the shooter went into the house, the killer had somehow disabled the alarm system, or he knew how to turn it off. Either that, or the alarm had been off from the beginning. The alarm company reported that the alarm was in perfect order. If Doris Angleton had set it before taking her daughters to the softball game, that meant the shooter almost certainly had to know how to disable the alarm, and more importantly, had to know how to *enable* it—otherwise it would have been disengaged when Doris had arrived home, which might have warned Doris to get out of the house. Especially since, the detectives learned, the alarm had gone off a week earlier in what appeared to be an aborted burglary attempt that had made Doris more than usually cognizant of setting the alarm when she went out.

Fact four: Who would know the alarm codes? Doris, of course, but she was dead. Who else, then? What about the dead woman's husband—Bob?

Fact five: Bob's strange tale the night before to Detective Wright, in which Bob had first told Wright that he worked for the police department, and then admitted that he was a bookmaker who was also an informant for the HPD's vice unit. That had been the reason Bob had at first refused to allow the search; he'd been afraid that the police would find evidence linking him to the bookmaking. Presumably, Tyson had told him that being arrested for bookmaking was the least of his worries at that point, with Doris lying dead inside the house. And then Bob had suggested that perhaps other bookmakers might be responsible for Doris' death in retaliation for his work against them with HPD's vice squad.

Well, what *about* Bob? He had the alibi, of course, but in something like this, that didn't mean anything.

"A situation like this, you always look at the husband first," Ferguson was to say later in his laconic Louisiana drawl, and that's just what he and Novak did.

Just as Ferguson and Novak were reviewing what was known about Doris Angleton's murder, so was Bob. He was meeting in a west Houston lawyer's office with his attorney, George Tyson, and his control with the HPD, vice officer Kevin Templeton.

Templeton was 42, a nineteen-year veteran of the Houston Police Department. In 1993, he was honored as a nationally recognized expert on gambling and crime. As Bob's control, it was Templeton's job to obtain information from Bob on who was conducting illegal bookmaking operations in the city, and to use that information to shut the operations down and arrest the bookmakers.

Later, Templeton would acknowledge that Bob was a "problem informant," meaning that to the HPD vice squad, it was as likely that Bob was breaking the law as helping to enforce it, but in the department's view, his contributions to vice enforcement outweighed the damage caused by his own violations. In effect, Templeton preferred to ignore Bob's activities as long as Bob continued to provide Templeton with information on others, rationalizing that it was better to know exactly who was in business and having some chance at controlling them rather than have a number of other unknown bookmakers at work in places the police could only guess at. It was an enforcement strategy that was to create considerably heated controversy within HPD as the investigation of Doris Angleton's murder unfolded.

But on this day, April 17, Templeton was less concerned about bookmaking than he was about whether Doris' murder might be related to Bob's activities as Templeton's informant, and what the crime might portend to Bob's continued usefulness to Templeton in maintaining tabs on the illegal bookmaking community. In short, Templeton's star snitch might be in double jeopardy—if not from some revenge-minded bookmaker, then maybe even from the HPD itself as it considered whether Bob was involved in the murder.

Just after noon, Templeton called the HPD homicide office. Novak picked up the call. Templeton told Novak that he and Bob were in George Tyson's office discussing who might have a motive for killing Doris. After some discussion about other bookmakers, Templeton brought up another possibility: Bob's own brother, Roger.

Novak inquired: Who is this Roger, and why might he be a suspect? Bob had said nothing about any Roger the night before with Wright.

Roger was Bob's older brother, from San Diego, California, Templeton explained, adding that it appeared that Roger had been trying to extort money from Bob.

Extortion? What's all this about extortion? Novak wanted to know.

Bob recently got an extortion note from Roger, Templeton said, demanding $200,000 in cash, and promising that if Bob didn't turn over the money, Roger would come to Houston and make Bob pay "dearly."

An extortion note from Bob's own brother? That sounded pretty squirrelly to Novak. But even more bothersome was Templeton's presence at Tyson's office with Bob, someone who had to be considered a possible suspect in Doris' murder. That spoke to Novak of a relationship between Bob and Kevin Templeton that might not be in HPD's best interests, especially if Templeton was helping Bob work out alternative scenarios to explain Doris' murder.

Novak told Templeton to come in to the homicide office—alone. And bring the note with you, he added.

Early that afternoon Templeton, accompanied by his own sergeant, arrived at the sixth-floor offices of the homicide division at HPD headquarters in downtown Houston. Novak, Ferguson, and the supervising lieutenant of the homicide unit met with him, and he provided the note.

Handwritten on broad-ruled paper that appeared to have been torn from a composition notebook, the note was short and to the point:

> Bob [it read],
>   After seeing you last week, my position remains the same & it is final . . . $200,000.00 in cash or I will hurt you in a way that will be with you for the rest of your life . . . I have nothing to lose.
>   If I don't hear fr. you agreeing to the $200K, I am coming there & will make you pay dearly. I am not kidding! Call me by March 20th.
>   I won't meet you alone so don't think up any tricks. If you don't call me at [a San Diego phone number] very soon and agree to this, it will be too late and everybody will lose.
>
> Roger

When did Bob get this note? Novak and Ferguson asked.

Bob had said early in March, Templeton told them. How did it come?

By mail, Templeton said. Bob said he threw away the envelope it came in.

Had Bob paid the money?

No, Templeton said. He got mad and refused.

Templeton went on to sketch in the outlines of his relationship with Bob, and what he knew about the Angleton brothers. Roger was older than Bob, and lived in San Diego. He was in real estate. Roger once worked for Bob, but Bob had fired him. After being fired, Roger had threatened to expose Bob's bookmaking activities to the federal government. As a result, Bob and Roger had worked out some sort of arrangement in which Bob had agreed to give Roger some money. The arrangement had been negotiated between lawyers for both brothers. Bob's lawyer was the former head of the district attorney's special investigations section—the people who handled vice prosecutions.

Novak and Ferguson weren't sure what to make of this story. Was it likely that Bob's own brother had killed Bob's wife to punish him for not giving him still more money? That Roger had made good on a written threat to Bob to "make you pay dearly"? And that Bob had saved this note, and had simply forgotten to mention it the night before, when talking to Wright?

One thing was sure, and that was that more conversation with Bob was needed. They asked Templeton to arrange for Bob to come in to be interviewed. Templeton returned to his own desk and began writing a lengthy report about Bob's bookmaking activities, the cases he had worked on, people who might have a grudge against him, and Bob's relationship with Roger. Eventually the report would go to homicide.

Later that afternoon, Bob arrived at the homicide office with Tyson.

Bob and Tyson spent a number of hours with Novak and Ferguson, as Bob went over the events of the night before, and following this, some details of his relationship with Roger. Bob's statement was not tape-recorded, so a verbatim record of it does not exist. It's likely, however, that it was at this point that Bob first told the Houston Police Department that a divorce with Doris was pending, a fact he'd apparently neglected to tell Wright the night before. In addition to the sudden appearance of brother Roger in the mix, Bob now said that the upstairs safe—the one that he had said the night before was usually open—had been broken into, and $10,000 in cash was missing.

After several hours of conversation, including a run-down on his activities for the vice squad, Bob was free to leave. A written statement would be prepared, Bob was told, and he would be invited back to review it, and if it was accurate, to sign it.

Almost as soon as Bob had left, however, Novak and Ferguson got on the telephone to authorities in San Diego, "just to see if [Bob] was BS-ing us," as Ferguson put it later, about brother Roger.

That was when the detectives learned that Roger Nicholas Angleton did indeed exist, that he had a criminal record in San Diego, and that he was wanted for failing to appear in court on drug-related charges on April 16—the very day that Doris had been murdered.

THE ANGLETONS

NINE

Later, authorities in Houston were to assemble only the most cursory information on the distant past of the Brothers Angleton. As Ferguson later put it, the detectives weren't really all that interested in the psychodynamics of two brothers and how they had come to be the way they were; what the police wanted to find out was whether Bob had conspired with his brother to murder his wife, or if this was some crazy plot that Roger had cooked up on his own.

One thing was clear to the detectives: It wasn't likely that Doris' murder was the work of some revenge-bent, Bob-busted bookie, or of some other sinister force, such as the Mob; in that case, why go after Doris instead of Bob himself? The seeming absence of evidence of burglary or robbery, coupled with the number of times Doris had been shot, seemed to indicate a more personal motive.

Detectives Novak and Ferguson did learn that Roger and Bob both had the same middle name: Nicholas. Roger was born in 1942, which made him six years older than Bob, who was born in 1948. Both brothers had been born in New Jersey, where they'd grown up, as was apparent from their East Coast accents and their almost staccato method of speaking.

Both brothers had gone into sales, and had moved to Florida by the early 1970s, where both had married, Robert to an airline stewardess named Lollie. Ferguson later discovered that both brothers had been involved in some sort of restaurant business in Florida for a while; the restaurant had gone under..

The brothers seemed to have arrived in Houston in the middle to late 1970s, where Bob went into the used-car business, and Roger had gone into real estate.

Of the two brothers, Bob seemed by far the more organized, almost a classic Type A personality, focused on his goals, as well as being both brash and commanding, almost dictatorial; whereas Roger seemed disorganized, a plunger given to flights of melodrama, as if life were a movie and he was the star.

Later, some would call Roger a lunatic, and even Bob's lawyers would try to cast him as desperate and deranged. Crazy or not, at the very least Roger was demonstrably eccentric, as later events showed. The two disparate personalities of Roger and Bob eventually were to form the crux of the dispute over what actually happened to Doris Angleton on the night she was murdered, as both the police and Bob's own lawyers soon realized.

Perhaps the best look at the Angletons, however—including Doris—would eventually be published in *Texas Monthly,* a regional glossy magazine focused on art, politics, and culture in the Lone Star State.

In a piece titled "The Bookmaker's Wife," contributing editor Skip Hollandsworth burrowed into the life and times of Doris, Bob, and Roger, and emerged with a compelling portrait of a woman on the edge of profound change, her relationship with her rigid and controlling husband, and in turn, her husband's relationship with his flamboyant, unpredictable brother.

"The Bookmaker's Wife" was set against a lush background of easy money, high times, and the social cachet of Houston's upwardly mobile baby boomer set—marked by expensive dinners in exclusive restaurants, evenings in trendy clubs, and augmented by social interactions where a wink, a handshake, a nod, told both deliverer and receiver that they had reached the promised land.

Published in November 1997, three months after the brothers were charged with killing Doris, Hollandsworth's article drew upon a broad range of anecdotes from friends of Doris and acquaintances of Bob and Roger, along with perhaps the only detailed interview ever given by Bob, conducted in the Harris County jail by Hollandsworth, with Bob's lawyer Michael Ramsey in attendance.

Among other things during his two-month investigation, Hollandsworth was to discover that Doris Angleton had been having a secret affair in the months before her murder, a fact that Bob almost certainly knew or at least suspected, as the police eventually concluded.

According to Bob via Hollandsworth in the interview, Roger and Bob were the sons of a Greek cabin boy,

Nicholas Angletos, who jumped ship in the small Texas seaport of Port Lavaca sometime in the 1920s. Nicholas changed Angletos for Angleton, went to the East Coast, married, and went into the construction business building barracks for the government in World War II; he eventually branched into building garden apartments in New Jersey after the war. As a result, Nicholas Angleton became quite successful, and the Brothers Angleton grew up in an atmosphere of wealth, even luxury.

As Hollandsworth in his article described the brothers' upbringing, Roger and Bob grew up in a large home, surrounded by an acre and a half of land. During the summers, the family often returned to Greece, and sailed the Mediterranean aboard a large yacht.

During his forty-five-minute interview with Hollandsworth, Bob described his older brother as very bright but undisciplined, and something of a source of consternation to his parents, wrecking cars, getting thrown out of various schools, and eventually being sent to a New York military academy as a means of discipline.

Bob, in contrast, told of no youthful hijinks, and said he'd attended Syracuse University, where he majored in philosophy. The differences between the brothers could not have been made more stark: Wild Man Roger, wrecker of cars and schools, and his younger brother, Bob, the obedient, contemplative, cerebral student. To some extent, the characterizations offered to Hollandsworth foreshadowed the defense strategy eventually adopted by defense lawyer

Ramsey when Bob was brought to trial; given that this story of the two brothers' past was provided by Bob when he was under indictment for murder, and preparing to blame his brother for all that had befallen him, one might expect to encounter at least some exaggeration, at least as to Roger's antics, Bob's placid youth, or the family's reputed wealth. Still, it was quite true that Bob attended Syracuse; the university later confirmed that Bob had graduated in 1971 with a bachelor's degree in arts and sciences; and Hollandsworth, in his efforts to verify Bob's version, eventually concluded that much of what Bob said about Roger was true: Roger's own behavior in Houston in the 1980s demonstrated that he was, in Hollandsworth's words, "a goofball."

In any event, according to Hollandsworth, neither brother was interested in joining their father in his construction business. Moreover, Bob apparently broke with his father over his marriage to Lollie, the airline stewardess. Shortly thereafter, the two brothers made the move to Florida, where the restaurant venture was begun, and eventually folded, precipitating the move to Texas.

In the 1970s, Texas was in the midst of a huge boom, fueled by the astronomic rise in oil prices flowing out of the Arab oil embargo of 1973. By the latter part of the decade, hundreds of thousands of Northerners had moved to Texas to try to cash in.

Bob went into the used-car business, while Roger went into real estate. At first Roger appeared to be the more successful, moving to the top of a well-known real-estate business in the Galleria area, netting tens of thousands in commissions from the pricey real estate in the city's most desirable section. Times weren't as good for Bob, however.

"Bob came first," Hollandsworth said, "and he was like a lot of the Northerners: He didn't know any of the Texas boys, he didn't have any connections. Then Roger came, and he figured out how to cash in on the boom, with the real estate."

Just how much Roger's initial success in real estate and Bob's relative lack of it in used cars may have affected the subsequent events can't be said with certainty; it is nevertheless true that the two brothers' relationship over the following two decades was to display all the classic signs of a virulent sibling rivalry.

But if Roger was initially successful selling real estate in the booming Texas market of the 1970s and early 1980s, Bob had his own ideas on how to get rich.

As Hollandsworth later pieced together the story, it was sometime in the late 1970s or early 1980s when a banker Bob had been using to finance his customers' car loans made him an offer: Would Bob like to open a sideline, make a little extra cash?

The banker was a bookie.

TEN

Later, while Bob declined to discuss anything about illegal betting with Hollandsworth, so much was to emerge about Bob's career as a bet broker (and as an HPD informant) that it came to seem that the only

people in Houston who *didn't* know that Bob was
booking was, well, the FBI.

In actuality, Bob's gambling prosperity was known
to only a handful of his non-betting acquaintances
during the 1980s and 1990s, with the exception of a
few select members of the Houston Police Department.

But by the time Hollandsworth's piece emerged in
Texas Monthly in November 1997, Bob's history as
a bookmaker had already received heavy play in the
Houston area news media. Hollandsworth took the
story to another level, however, when he was able to
track down and interview the banker who had given
Bob his start as a booker of bets.

As it happened, Hollandsworth was on good terms
with a number of old college friends from the Wichita
Falls area of north Texas; these friends in turn introduced him to the often subterranean world of bookies
and bettors.

"I'd never bet with a bookie in my life," Hollandsworth was to recall later. But falling in with his
old cronies, many of whom were young, single, and
looking for action, Hollandsworth soon found himself
hanging out in a number of bars along Houston's
Richmond Avenue inside the West Loop. At a place
with a giant saxophone on the roof, Hollandsworth
was introduced to Bob's old buddy the banker, who
then told Hollandsworth just how he'd broken Bob
into the bookie business.

The bookmaking racket as conducted today is a far
cry from the way it's often portrayed in film noir;

rather than a seedy operation run by cigar-chomping men in green eyeshades furtively whispering horse race odds into a columnar telephone behind bolted doors, a modern bookmaker has far more in common with a stock brokerage or insurance business. In all three cases, the profit comes from the normal ten-percent commission—"the vig," or, "the juice," as it's referred to in the betting business. Moreover, virtually all bookmaking in the United States today consists of wagers on college and professional sports, usually football and basketball, rather than horse racing.

If, for example, a bettor wished to wager $100 on the outcome of an athletic contest—say the University of Texas against Oklahoma, or the Dallas Cowboys against the New York Giants—all he had to do was telephone the bookie, provide his customer identification number, and put down the bet. It was understood that as of that moment, the bettor owed the bookie $110—$100 for the wager, $10 for the commission.

To keep the book balanced—that is, even between winners and losers—the bookie manipulated "the line." If a thousand bettors wagered $100 each on the University of Texas, for example, and none on Oklahoma, the book stood to lose $100,000 if Texas won. To balance the book, the bookie provided an inducement for bettors to bet on Oklahoma—a number of points that Texas would have to win by in order for the bettor to win.

This was "the line"—say, eight points, or some such similar amount calculated to attract an equal number of bettors to either side of the wager. Thus, if the University of Texas defeated the University of Oklahoma by a score of 20-14, and the line was eight points, those who had bet on Texas would still lose, since Texas did not win by eight or more points.

In Houston, as it is everywhere else in the country, "the line" is initially set in Las Vegas, where such sports betting is completely legal. The line on any number of sports events, but most prominently college and professional football and basketball, is publicized in most major newspapers across the country each week; most illegal bookmakers begin with the Las Vegas line.

As the week progresses, and as the bookie's clientele make their wagers, the bookie's book may become overbalanced on one side or the other. To keep his book in balance, a local bookie may make small local adjustments in the line; thus, the line on Texas might be slightly higher in Houston than in Norman, Oklahoma, because more bettors in Houston might have a natural predisposition to support their home-state team; meanwhile, bettors in Oklahoma might have a similar predisposition for *their* own team.

Finally, as the day and time of the game nears, the bookie may take a last-minute rush of bets, always keeping conscious of the status of the book, trying to keep it in balance. At the very last minute, a bookie may in fact make his own bet with another bookie in order to achieve this balance; this is called "laying off," essentially, hedging or reinsuring to cover all the bets. A Houston bookie, for instance, might call a Norman bookie and place a large bet at the higher

Norman point spread in order to keep his accounts in balance.

Once the game is over, along with all the other games offered by the bookie, the winnings and losings are toted up; this is called "recapping" the book. The winning $100 bettor is then paid an equal amount by the bookie. If the bookie is doing his job right, the money for the winners should come from the losers; where the bookie makes money is from the ten-percent commission—$10 from each $100 bettor, both winners and losers, and more, as the size of the bet goes up.

Just as stockbrokers and insurance brokers have employees, so do bookmakers. In the bookie business, the "agent" is generally the point of contact between the bettor and the owner of the book. It's the agent who manages the individual bettor's account, who passes the line on, who arranges to collect the bet and pay off the winnings.

Like his counterparts in the stock and insurance businesses, the bookmaker's agent is a sort of amalgam of a salesman and an accountant. Drawing on his circle of acquaintances, both in business and in his social circle, the agent books the bets and services the bettors, always taking care to let the supervising bookmaker know the status of the betting, i.e., whether it's in or out of balance. A large-scale bookmaker may have a fairly large number of such agents reporting to him, each passing the ten-percent "juice" further up the line, less, of course, the agent's piece of the action. To complicate matters even further, some agents become bookies in their own right, with their own separate bettors, along with the bettors they may service for a superior.

In this way, the bookmaking business also has something in common with franchising; having the capacity to "lay off" to someone further up the line helps keep an agent solvent, and therefore, in the minds of bettors, more reliable.

When the banker-bookie offered Bob the chance to join the party, it was an opportunity for Bob to exit the low-margin business of used cars and get into Houston's fast lane. Bob was well suited to the task: His years of sales experience, his glib East Coast patter, and his quick brain were almost perfect for the bookmaking business.

Within a short time, the used-car business was liquidated, and Bob soon moved into booking full-time; by the early 1980s, Bob was making a significant amount of money for his banker pal and his partners. Bob began hanging out among the trendier spots inside the West Loop, glib, witty, slightly acerbic, a social anomaly among the down-home boys, but definitely a mover to watch.

Watching Bob was exactly what a Houston Police Department vice officer named Wes Fielder was doing by 1985. As Bob's circle of acquaintances and clients grew, as his action with the banker-bookie and the banker-bookie's other partner grew, Bob grew ever more prosperous, and thus, more conspicuous. Eventually, Fielder arrested Bob, according to Hollandsworth, although there is no court record of the arrest.

Fielder was a veteran vice officer, and knew well how the game was played. It was Fielder's job to spot people like Bob, arrest them, and then induce the collaree to trade up—to inform on those higher up the gambling food-chain.

Exactly what transpired between Fielder and Bob has never been made public and remains a matter of confidential police records—if indeed any written records exist at all. But Hollandsworth's source, the banker-bookie who gave Bob his start, soon himself was busted by the police. The banker-bookie told Hollandsworth that he was convinced that Bob had set him up for Fielder to get out from under his own arrest.

"I think that's when the turn was made," Hollandsworth said later. "That's when Bob went from being an agent for a bookie to being the bookie himself. The banker knew that Bob had been arrested. Every day he'd ask him, 'What's going on with your case?' Finally, Bob told him, 'Oh, I've worked something out.'"

What the banker-bookie was, was out of business.

As it later emerged—in reports by the *Houston Chronicle,* Hollandsworth's *Texas Monthly,* and eventually, in an internal investigation by the Houston Police Department itself—Bob soon became Fielder's champion informer.

Hollandsworth talked to a number of Houston bookies who had an idea of how things worked: After Bob had knocked off the banker-bookie and had taken over his business, he used the lay-off procedure to identify other bookies, simultaneously building them up while taking their measure. When they'd reached a certain ripeness, Bob would pluck them from the tree, turning the identity of the bookie over to the police, then moving in on the busted bookie's customers.

According to the bookies interviewed by *Chronicle* reporters and Hollandsworth, this happened again and again throughout the 1980s and even into the 1990s. Eventually, it even happened to Fielder, of all people, when Fielder retired from the police department and went into the bookmaking business for himself. The other bookies claim that Bob had done in his old police partner just the same way he had done them.

Later, when all this came out in the aftermath of Doris' murder, Bob was to deny ever having been an informant; that denial eventually became inoperative as the Angleton case progressed, however, as the extent of Bob's relationship with Fielder and later Kevin Templeton came to light.

In any event, by the mid-1990s, Bob's bookmaking business had prospered wildly; some were to estimate that the total amount bet annually with Bob was anywhere between $20 million and $40 million a year, and had among its clientele some of the wealthiest and most prominent people in Houston, with his name being whispered around some of Houston's most exclusive clubs.

Bob was particularly successful with rich University of Texas fraternity boys; he reasoned that at some time in the future, these neophytes would have the money and position to be the backbone of his business. Hollandsworth was told that Bob had up to twenty agents working for him; Bob paid each a retainer that averaged $2,000 a month, along with a rent-free apartment and free color television, Hollandsworth said his sources told him.

In short, Bob had become Houston's biggest and most successful bookmaker, albeit with the assistance, witting or no, of the police department.

Whether this cozy relationship with the police made Bob even more confident and brash than he normally was isn't certain; what is known is that he soon developed a grating Yankee superiority over his Texas clientele.

As Hollandsworth put it in *Texas Monthly,* "Angleton would call a bettor who had just lost a big bet to him and crow, 'Hey there, lucky!'

" 'You'd get so pissed off at him,' " Hollandsworth wrote that a former gambler told him, " 'that you'd double up your bets the next day just to try to beat him.' "

But Bob was crafty. He seemed to know just how to keep the book balanced, constantly adjusting the line for up to forty games, always striving to keep the customers coming back on both sides, collecting the juice all the way. Bob constantly juggled a collection of cellular telephones and pagers, keeping on top of the line, working his book, keeping it balanced. Bob had a sharply honed instinct for the numbers of betting; some people, in fact, considered him "the human calculator."

"One thing you had to say about him," a gambler

told Hollandsworth, "was that he knew how to make money."

And as it turned out, apart from his police connections, his brashness, and his smarts, Bob had one more thing going for him: Doris McGown Beck, eventually Doris Angleton.

ELEVEN

Sometime in late 1979 or early 1980, Bob was attending a party in a fashionable bar someplace inside the West Loop when he encountered a beautiful 28-year-old woman, and was immediately smitten: This was, as Bob later told Hollandsworth with tears in his eyes, the woman he intended to marry.

There were two immediate problems with this scenario: one, Bob was already married, to Lollie; and second, Doris was already married, to William Beck.

That didn't matter to Bob.

As the story later came to Detectives Ferguson and Novak—repeated as it was among many of the denizens of the River Oaks set after Doris' murder—Bob took one look at Doris and told Bill Beck that if he ever wanted to split up with Doris, Bob would be more than happy to take her off his hands.

Hollandsworth's version of the story is much the same, only perhaps more vivid: Approaching Beck, Bob told him, "Anytime you decide to get rid of that pretty lady, I want to know about it."

This seems to have been vintage Bob: direct, blunt, even a little vulgar, as if Doris were some sort of prize, or even a used car with high book value.

"I was rough around the edges, no question about it," Bob told Hollandsworth in his interview.

But it appeared that each brought something to the match that the other either lacked or wanted; for Bob, Doris was class personified, easy in her relations with the River Oaks crowd, socially skilled where Bob was almost involuntarily abrasive. Doris was Bob's passport to social circles he might never reach on his own.

At the same time, Bob held a sort of fascination for Doris: a large man, quick-witted, slightly dangerous, with a cachet of the risk-taker so esteemed along Buffalo Bayou.

"She was used to the typical Texans," Bob told Hollandsworth, "and she liked meeting someone who was a doer—a nonstop doer."

Doris McGown was born April 11, 1951, the oldest child of Ann McGown and her husband, Randy, a Dow Chemical engineer. The McGowns lived in Lake Jackson, a small town not far from Galveston.

From her earliest childhood, Doris was bright, engaging, and sociable—almost as if she'd been born with a gene that gifted her in getting along with people. Her greatest strength was in feeling—to sense, somehow, where others were, and to reach out to them for inclusion.

When she was a bit over three years old, Doris heard that the similarly-aged daughter of the neighbors across the street had a new little brother. Doris wanted one, too.

"I'm going to have a little brother," the precocious Doris would tell people, whereupon Randy and Ann would say that Doris knew something that was news to them. But a year or so later, Steve McGown came into the world, exactly as Doris had predicted.

As Doris grew older, she became very protective of her little brother, making sure to include him in outings and finding time to play with him. By the time she was in high school and dating, Doris even convinced some of her dates to include Steve when they went out.

As a result, Doris and Steve were quite close, and generally confided in one another right up to the day she died.

"The biggest thing about Doris," Steve said later, "is that everybody knew when she was around, they were going to have fun. She was always upbeat, didn't waste time complaining, always doing things that were fun. She was always ready to do some sort of adventure at the drop of a hat. She wasn't looking for trouble, but she just had a knack for making people comfortable. She remembered things about people, even people she hadn't seen for years, and she'd include them in a way that made people feel good."

After graduating from the University of Texas with a degree in speech pathology, Doris became a schoolteacher for a few years. While she enjoyed being around children, she wasn't that happy with the money a public school teacher is paid. Doris then took a job as a sales representative for a large pharmaceutical company, where her sunny personality made her very successful.

Sometime in 1976, Doris met Bill Beck, who was a manufacturer's representative for a large office products firm. The two married and soon were living in Clear Lake, a Houston suburb.

While Steve McGown wasn't sure why his sister's marriage to Bill ended, Hollandsworth did find a friend of Doris who had a theory: Doris was bored in the suburbs. Drawn to the faster crowd inside the West Loop, Doris began to worry that life was passing her by.

"You could tell she was looking for something more exciting," the friend told Hollandsworth.

That was about the time that Doris first met Bob Angleton, then in his early thirties: a big man, six feet tall, nearly 200 pounds, flashing dark eyes, and an even flashier bankroll.

"I don't think there was a man who met her who didn't fall a little bit in love with her," one of Doris' longtime male friends told Hollandsworth. It was more than just Doris' striking good looks, it was the way she made people feel. Doris seemed to be "incorrigibly convivial," as Hollandsworth put it.

Bob pursued Doris with all the tenacity he might have employed for a heavy bettor, or previously on a hot used-car prospect. By early 1982, Bob had persuaded Doris to have dinner with him at Ruggles, a popular Houston restaurant.

It was as if Bob sensed in Doris the perfect antidote to his abrasive Eastern personality. With Doris on his arm, Bob had a sort of entree to Houston circles he might never have gained access to; people might not like Bob, but they accepted him because of Doris. She was a very visible and socially effective testament to Bob's success.

"It was his money and her personality," was how Hollandsworth put it.

Later, the Houston police detectives and the prosecutors in the Harris County district attorney's office were to be unanimous about Bob.

"We did not talk to one person during this whole investigation who had one positive thing to say about Bob," Dave Ferguson said later. "And I've never worked a murder case where that has ever occurred. I mean, normally someone has something good to say about the individual. But with Bob, we didn't find one person who had anything good to say about him."

The same point was made by Assistant District Attorneys Ted Wilson and Lyn McClellan, the men who eventually would prosecute Bob for murder.

"I never talked to anybody who didn't like Doris," Wilson said. "Even people who weren't involved with the case, people who knew her casually, like at her gym, they all liked Doris, but I never talked to one person who liked Bob."

"I defy you to go around and find friends of Bob's that are not economically connected to him," McClellan added. "You know, find somebody that doesn't have anything to do with him, economically, and is his friend. I don't know if you can turn up even one."

Well, Doris, at least, liked Bob; in the early 1980s, her brother Steve recalled, she was "very taken with

him.'' There was something exotic about the East-
erner with the fast mouth and the knack for making
money, so different from the usual laid-back Texans.

Early in 1982, Bob gave Doris a large diamond
engagement ring, the first of many gifts of jewelry
Bob would shower on Doris throughout their marriage; indeed, one of Doris' friends later discovered
that Doris had a literal embarassment of riches from
Bob.

"Doris had to stop telling Bob that she liked the
jewelry she saw on other women, because whenever
she did, he would immediately go out and find the
same jewelry for her,'' one of Doris' friends told
Hollandsworth.

Later, others saw this seemingly compulsive
jewelry-giving as Bob's attempt to mark Doris as his
property, a statement in gold and precious stones that
he was a man who could afford the very best.

In any event, Bob and Doris were soon moving
with the West Loop crowd, forming a supper club
with other young couples, and eventually joining the
Briar Club, an exclusive tennis and swim club in the
West Loop area. Bob's popular wife helped Bob gain
even more new customers for his book.

Then, on August 1, 1984, Doris gave birth to
twins: Nicole Anastasia, and Alessandra Elizabeth,
who soon came to be called Niki and Ali.

As the 1980s progressed, so did Bob's book. By
the middle of the decade, Bob and Doris moved to a
house in the comfortable Houston suburb of Bellaire,
where a frequent visitor was Bob's brother, Roger
Angleton.

TWELVE

If things were going well for Bob in the 1980s, the opposite was true for Roger as the oil boom busted.

With real estate on the rocks, Roger was having trouble making ends meet; Roger's wife left him. By 1989, Roger was nearly broke, and Bob decided to let his older brother in on the bookmaking bonanza, in addition to letting him live in Bob's Houston condo.

"I planned to teach him everything," Bob told Hollandsworth. "But he couldn't do the work. He didn't have a mind for it."

Ferguson later discovered that Roger had trouble keeping his part of the book balanced; that exposed Bob to risks, especially if he didn't find out about the imbalance in time to lay off with another bookie.

Bob finally fired Roger in August of 1990, thus precipitating a chain of events that some would later contend ended in Doris' murder seven years later.

In retrospect, Roger was a completely different sort of personality than Bob. Where Bob was cold, even calculating in his relationships, Roger tended to be extravagant. Bob had no interest in small talk, and was often brusque, even rude. Roger, on the other hand, was voluble, and often funny.

Roger had no reluctance to call attention to himself. He was famous in Houston for his Halloween costumes. One year, he showed up at a Halloween party for Ali and Niki dressed as a giant rabbit; an-

other year, he came as a rag doll. But when Bob fired
Roger from the book, Roger put on a different kind
of costume altogether: He became an extortionist.

As Bob later told the story to Ferguson and Novak—
as well as *Texas Monthly*'s Hollandsworth—Roger
thought his brother owed him something for the new
business Roger had brought to the book.

According to Bob, Roger tried to rob him.

It was in December of 1990. Bob was about to
close on a real estate deal that had been arranged by
Roger. The deal required Bob to bring $200,000 in
cash to a parking lot on Houston's west side, a fact
known to Roger, who was to participate in the closing. Bob had the money in a paper bag on the back
seat of his car.

When Bob pulled into the parking lot, Roger was
waiting for him. He got into the back seat of Bob's
car and asked Bob if he had the money.

"Yes," Bob said.

With that, Roger put his left arm around Bob's
throat and with his right hand pressed a stun gun to
Bob's neck. Bob heard the stun gun make a noise
and in the same instant, Bob threw his right elbow
back into Roger's face. Blood spurted around inside
the car.

Bob jumped out of the vehicle. Roger's face was
covered with blood. Roger got out of the car, too.

"I want the money," Roger said. He put his hand
in his coat pocket. Bob thought he had a gun.

To Bob, it appeared that Roger's eyes were glazed.
He kept repeating that he wanted the money.

You can have the money, Bob said he told Roger.

Roger backed around the car, still facing Bob. He saw a briefcase on the front passenger floor of the car. As Roger reached the opposite side of the car, Bob suddenly jumped back in behind the wheel, threw the car into reverse, and hit the gas pedal. When Bob looked back at Roger, his brother was pointing a pistol at him. Bob drove off.

Bob called Doris and told her what happened. While he was talking to Doris on his car phone, Roger called Doris on another line. According to Doris, Roger warned Bob not to tell anyone what happened in the parking lot if he didn't want to be exposed as a bookmaker.

Not long after, Doris agreed to meet with Roger. She went to the meeting with a friend. Roger told Doris that Bob owed him money from his bookmaking stint, and that if Bob didn't pay up, he'd send a "trunkful" of documentation on Bob's bookmaking to the authorities.

Even worse, from Bob's point of view, Roger began calling some of Bob's clients, pretending he was from the IRS, and asking pointed questions about the clients' betting. This was bad; if left unresolved, it could ruin the business.

Now Bob began a series of negotiations with Roger, using first a therapist that both brothers knew, and later Doris. Doris went to a meeting with Roger at a Houston restaurant wearing a tape recorder. At this meeting Roger threatened to kill Bob if he didn't get paid. Doris' friend told Bob that Roger was crazy.

In the end, Bob agreed to pay Roger $72,000—

$12,000 down and $2,500 a month, in exchange for the "trunkful" of documentation.

This deal between Bob and Roger was negotiated with the assistance of two Houston lawyers, and actually resulted in a written agreement signed by both brothers. Roger took the money and moved to San Diego, where both Doris and Bob hoped he would remain.

This appears to have been the last contact between Bob and his brother until early 1997, although Niki Angleton was later to say she had once seen Uncle Roger hanging around her school yard in perhaps 1994 or 1995. Both girls knew that something bad had happened between their father and their uncle, and knew that the subject of Roger distressed Doris.

Early in 1991, Doris and her mother went to Bob's Houston condo, the one Roger had been living in while he was working for Bob. They found that the place was riddled with bullet holes, between fifty and a hundred of them—apparently Roger's idea of revenge on his brother.

THIRTEEN

By the early 1990s, Bob's book had grown so well that he could afford to move his family into the River Oaks area. He bought a two-story brick Tudor on Ella Lee Lane, in the same neighborhood where the movie *Terms of Endearment* was filmed; the house in 1998 was worth more than $600,000. There was a beach house in Galveston as well.

Bob also had a number of legitimate businesses besides the book: the courier service, a small shopping mall in the West Loop, and an interest in a golf course west of the city.

Ali and Niki were enrolled in an exclusive private school, Annunciation Orthodox, as were the children of many of their River Oaks friends.

"It was very much a rich baby boomer kind of crowd," Hollandsworth said. "It was a very insular community, people who hung out at all the same restaurants, the club, the Astros—that kind of thing."

Doris rarely discussed Bob's business, particularly with strangers. But Doris really had very little interest in what Bob did to earn money, according to her brother.

"Doris didn't really know, didn't want to know," Steve McGown said. "She thought the less she knew, the better."

Whenever he visited his sister, Steve said, Bob was usually busy working.

"We'd go down to the beach house, and Bob would come in for dinner, then he'd be off to work again," Steve said. "He was always very busy."

For her part, Doris filled her hours with activities that centered on her family.

"She worked so hard at creating a normal life for her family," Doris' friend Mary Hill told Hollandsworth. "She volunteeered for everything at school, she threw a back-to-school party every October for the other moms, she decorated her house every holiday, she organized all the Girls' Nights Out."

Despite all the activities, friendships, and affluence, life with Bob wasn't easy.

Most of Doris' friends marveled at Doris' seeming acceptance of Bob's frequent criticisms of her; it was almost as if, having provided Doris with an opulent lifestyle, Bob felt he'd acquired the right to boss her around and tear at her self-esteem. Occasionally, Bob even humiliated Doris in public, calling her "stupid."

As the 1990s progressed, Bob seemed to become ever more obsessed in making money. To Doris, it was as if she had become just another object, another possession, of Bob's. Worse, in Doris' mind, Bob was becoming more and more controlling—giving her instructions, demanding that she account for her movements, telling her what to do and how to do it.

When she thought about what was missing in her life, Doris realized that for all her possessions, she lacked the one thing she wanted most—emotional intimacy with Bob. Doris, the girl with all the social graces, had locked herself into a marriage with a human calculator.

Doris needed to find a connection, some relationship with some person who would put feelings ahead of finances. Eventually, she would find one on the Internet; checking out an over-forty chat room on America Online, Doris, with her excellent social skills, made a number of new friends, including a man in New Jersey.

Her new friend seemed the antithesis of Bob: sensitive, cultured, empathetic, and definitely not bombastic or controlling.

By late 1996, Doris and the New Jersey man began meeting secretly, arranging rendezvous in Arizona, Austin, and on a trip to the Northeast.

Bob sensed Doris was pulling away. Doris confronted Bob with his controlling demeanor, demanding that Bob be more attuned to her and others' feelings. They began seeing a marriage counselor, but the sessions only seemed to confirm Doris in her feelings about Bob's behavior. The marriage entered a precarious state. Finally, in December of 1996, Doris resolved to see a divorce lawyer to consider her options. That was when she was referred to Tom Conner.

Bob, meanwhile, continued to try to win Doris back. He sent her flowers and left love notes under the windshield wipers of her car. He began talking about taking a long romantic trip with Doris to Italy in the spring, and began making plans for an April 11 birthday bash for Doris at Ruggles, the Houston restaurant where they'd had their first date.

But it was too late. By February, Doris had decided to go through with the divorce. Bob found out the hard way. He'd been trying to arrange to have country music singer Dwight Yoakum perform at Doris' birthday party. When Bob called the booking agency in Nashville, he was told that the performance would not be taking place "because of the pending divorce."

The papers were filed on February 7, 1997. Doris explained her reasons in a letter she wrote to Bob.

Dear Bob,

I'm writing this because I'm very afraid of what your reaction might be were I to tell you in person.

You won't be surprised to know that I don't feel we should go to the trip to Europe. You must know, since we haven't discussed it at all. I don't see how it can help things and it would be only one more painful expression of the sad plight in which we are involved. A trip is not going to take away the years of unhappiness. It will not heal the wounds.

I know how upsetting this must be for you, but let's face reality. In spite of the effort that has been put into this marriage by both of us, I think it is really over between us. I'm certain of it. Neither one of us can go on living this way. I know you are not happy either . . . and your needs are not being met.

I will always love and respect you as the father of my children. We will continue to share this for many years. I want you to share in that and I need your help. Our children need both of us.

But I'm ready to move on and I'm sure you are ready for something to happen. So I'm filing for divorce as of today. I retained a lawyer in December when things seemed so volatile and I didn't know what you were going to do next. I still feel that way, even though things have been calm lately, the undercurrent of volatility is still there and it is frightening.

The girls are my foremost concern in this and I hope yours as well. I don't want their lives to be ripped apart because we have our problems. We have to work this family thing out. I want you to take your time and find a place close . . . wait until after "GREASE," maybe while they are gone on spring break? I will move in the guest room or you can. Surely, we can work this out and make it as happy as it can be for THEM, as easy as it can be for THEM.

I have followed my attorney's advice. He's "enjoin-

*ing" the bank boxes if there are any, as I don't know
what steps you have already taken. He has assured me
that you have already probably taken steps.*

*After you read this, please take time to think about
it before you react. Then after you've thought, please
call, page me, and we can meet somewhere, and hope-
fully be able to discuss this sanely and rationally. I'm
sure you have some ideas, and have been thinking
along these lines for some time.*

I am just ready to move to the next step.

*Love,
Doris*

This was the pith of the message: Doris wanted
out.

Bob was devastated by Doris' determination to end
their marriage, according to his friends and acquaintances; suddenly, it was as if they were speaking different languages. And there were practical matters to
consider.

With the bank boxes frozen by court order, Bob
was cut off from a substantial portion of his working
capital. Something needed to be done, so Bob's lawyer worked out an amendment to Conner's court order, one that allowed Doris and Bob to go together
to the boxes and jointly open them.

This they did on February 27, when Doris and Bob
went to a branch of the Northern Trust bank and removed $3.2 million in cash. Doris and Bob then split
the money into two piles: his and hers.

Doris took her half and opened two new safe-
deposit boxes at Northern Trust, one accessible by
Doris and her mother, the other accessible by Doris
and her father. Doris put half of her $1.6 million into
each of the boxes.

FOURTEEN

Later, police and prosecutors were to contend that Bob was holding out on Doris, that there was more—much more—money in still other safe-deposit boxes. But however much money there was in however many boxes, there was a potential problem: the tax man.

Because of attorney-client confidentiality, Conner was unable to later say what advice he had given Doris. But as Conner later pointed out, Doris did go to see a tax lawyer at his suggestion: Ed Urquhart.

That visit was on April 10, the day before her birthday, and six days before she was shot dead.

Doris' visit to the tax lawyer was later to loom large in the minds of the police and Harris County district attorneys.

"Here's the bottom line," Lyn McClellan was to say later. "Doris had filed for divorce; he [Bob] by law would have to give up half of his assets to her; he'd given her $1.6 million and said that was half of the cash, although, of course after the fact, we found another $4 million that he somehow forgot to give her. And there's probably more than that. That's just stuff we stumbled on to.

"Then Urquhart's suggestion would probably be, in order to clean your money, you're going [to have] to report it to the IRS with an amended joint tax return, report this kind of stuff. What do you do now, [if] you're Bob Angleton? She's going to divorce you, she's already filed that. She's already frozen the safe-deposit boxes that she knew about, luckily she didn't know about them all.

"I'm out, tentatively, one and a half million. I'm going to have to end up giving up half of the house, have to give up half of everything I own. She gets half of everything, for someone who's divorcing *me*.

"Now, the kicker, though, is she wants to go file an amended tax return with the IRS, and the problem is, she doesn't even know the tip of the iceberg.

"If we start going over there [the IRS], they're not only going to want a bunch of that money, they're gonna want penalties, they're going to want interest, they're also gonna want some criminal liability, a little federal pen time there.

"Now, if Doris were to die, the divorce won't be granted, I mean, she won't be around; I won't have to give up half the assets, and I don't have to pay the IRS or do anything else, because nobody's going to find out about it."

That, then, was Bob's supposed motive in arranging the murder of his wife: She wanted to go straight, and it promised to cost him everything he had.

LOOKING FOR ROGER

FIFTEEN

On the day immediately after Doris' murder, as first Templeton and then Bob himself were interviewed by the homicide investigators, a great deal of this background information about Bob, Doris, and Roger had yet to be learned.

In his interview on April 17, Bob told Ferguson and Novak that after he'd paid Roger off in 1993, he had not seen or heard from his brother—until early in January of that year.

According to Bob, Roger was now up to his old tricks, again demanding money and threatening exposure of Bob to the authorities.

Bob said he'd received a brief note from Roger, demanding a meeting. Bob wrote Roger back, and provided his brother with telephone numbers where he could be reached. In the middle of February of 1997—around the time Bob was being served with the divorce papers—Roger called Bob on his cellular phone, and insisted on meeting Bob.

Bob agreed to meet with Roger at a Denny's restaurant.

"I drove to Denny's," Bob told the detectives. "Roger was at Denny's when I arrived. [He] was

outside standing by the front door, but I didn't recognize him at first.''

Roger went inside, and Bob followed him, now
recognizing his brother.

''Roger smelled of cigarette smoke, and he looked
old and worn down,'' Bob said.

The brothers went to a table in the back. They each
frisked the other for hidden recorders. Then Bob
asked Roger what he wanted.

He wanted $200,000, Roger said, to keep from
spilling the beans about the bookmaking business.

Bob got up from the table. He pulled $500 from
his pocket and threw it on the table.

''Go fuck yourself,'' Bob told Roger. ''That
should take care of your plane fare home.''

Bob walked out.

The next contact he'd had with Roger was when
he'd received the note that he'd given to Templeton
that morning, Bob said.

Ferguson took notes that would be used as the basis for a formal written statement for Bob to sign, one
about Roger, and the other about Bob's movements
and actions on the night of the murder.

At the end of the session, Novak asked Bob if he
were willing to take a polygraph test. Bob said he
was.

As things developed, however, the police never offered to conduct the test, according to Bob's lawyers.

After Bob and Tyson left, the homicide detectives
considered what to do next. Obviously, the first task
would be to locate Roger. If it turned out that Roger

had a solid alibi for the evening of April 16, that would tend to rule him out, despite Bob's extortion tales.

Ferguson and Novak were struck by the convenience of Roger's sudden appearance as Bob's bogeyman.

Asked if Bob had plotted with his brother to kill his wife, why he would then turn immediately around and name Roger as a suspect, Ferguson later said that he and Novak came to believe that this was a ploy by both brothers to direct the investigators away from Bob.

"First off, I thought, to get the police off his tail," Ferguson said later. "And put 'em on Roger's. But I think, I really think, they were so confident that they were going to get away with this . . . that they would not be caught, that—when you have a thing such as this, the number one suspect, after you look at insurance and things like that . . . I mean, admittedly, you're going to think the husband is going to be the suspect, so to throw the police off the husband, [it's] my brother did it. I've got the history, there's all these extortions, plots, blah blah blah. We still had Bob as a suspect, but I think that was their initial reason, to throw us off of Bob and on to Roger; and they just thought they would get away with this, and except for a couple of screwups by Roger, they would have."

In addition to discovering that Roger was AWOL from his drug trial in San Diego, the investigators soon learned that Roger had obtained a temporary

Texas driver's license in El Paso on February 26—about the time that Bob said he had met with Roger at Denny's.

Checking Roger's credit history also proved fruitful. The detectives discovered that Roger had booked into a Houston motel on March 5, and had left by March 7. Another visit to Houston by Roger took place in late March, as did a car rental; in fact, the detectives discovered that on March 23, Roger obtained a month's lease on an apartment not far from Bob's courier office.

This definitely seemed to indicate that Roger might have been in Houston on the night of the murder.

But as to Roger's current whereabouts, no one seemed to have a clue.

But then Roger was to commit what Ferguson was to call a screwup.

The man was in a hurry to get to Los Angeles. He approached an American Airlines ticket counter at the Dallas-Fort Worth airport. He wanted to pay cash for the ticket. The clerk was very helpful; since he was in such a hurry, did Mr. Tratora want to get an earlier flight? One was leaving in less than twenty minutes.

Sure, said Mr. Tratora.

Because the baggage had already been loaded on the flight, Mr. Tratora's suitcase would have to go on the plane as a carry-on. The ticket agent helped Mr. Tratora toward the gate. Arriving at the security detector, the agent swung the heavy suitcase onto the belt.

At that point, the security alarm went off. There, in the X-ray viewer of the detector were the unmistakable outlines of two pistols.

What's this? the security people wanted to know.

What's what? Mr. Tratora asked.

These guns, what about these guns? You can't bring these aboard the plane.

Mr. Tratora said he didn't know anything about them, and he started walking away from the detector, heading back toward the front of the terminal.

It's my brother's suitcase, they must be his guns, Mr. Tratora kept saying as he walked. Let me go get him, he's right out in front by the taxi stand. He'll explain.

The security guards told Mr. Tratora that he had to stay there while the suitcase was opened, but Mr. Tratora was already a long way toward the front door.

Stop. Wait, said the security people, but Mr. Tratora was already gone.

When the airport police opened the suitcase, they found, in addition to the two pistols, some sort of Greek identity document in the name of Roger Angleton, a microcassette recorder (empty) and a clipping from the *Houston Chronicle* reporting the murder of Doris Angleton five days earlier.

The next day, the Dallas-Fort Worth airport police called the Houston homicide detectives and told them about the strange Mr. Tratora, his guns, and his clipping.

Does this mean anything to you? the Dallas people asked.

Novak said it did indeed. A picture of Roger was sent to the airport police, who showed it to the airline and security people. Yes, everyone agreed, that was Mr. Tratora.

The following day Novak went to Dallas and picked up the suitcase. The hunt for Roger was on.

SIXTEEN

Just where Roger went immediately after abandoning his suitcase at the Dallas-Fort Worth airport remains unclear. What was clear at the time, however, was that Roger was using an alias, Frank Tratora; that, in turn, suggested that Roger knew he was wanted—a warrant for his arrest was outstanding in San Diego—and that he had made preparations to go underground.

When the suitcase was brought back to Houston and more closely examined, some new items within suggested their importance. One was a supply of .22-caliber ammunition, identical in type to the bullets used to snuff the life from Doris Angleton; another, more ominous, was a handwritten schedule of Doris' activities for the days before and after April 16. The handwriting appeared to be similar to that in the note that Roger had supposedly given to Bob in early March.

This seemed to be fairly significant evidence that Roger might have been involved in Doris' murder.

A canvas of various Houston area hotels and motels was undertaken that was to last for some time. Drawing on Roger's credit card records and his business activities in San Diego helped piece together some of his movements before the murder, but the fact that he now had at least one new name suggested that there might be others, as well as the fact that Roger knew he was hot.

This preparation for a clandestine lifestyle seems to have been a manifestation of one of Roger's eccentricities: a strong preoccupation with secret agent paraphernalia and spy techniques, such as disguises, false identities, codes, and surreptitious surveillance. Roger liked to think of himself as crafty, capable of disappearing whenever he wanted to, and practiced in the art of setting up cut-out communications, where a third party was used as a go-between. In addition, the suitcase also contained a number of weird items—a bottle and several boxes of hair dye, wigs, eyeglasses, two pairs of binoculars, a monocular, and a scanner radio, all of which seemed to suggest that Roger had made attempts to disguise himself while keeping someone under surveillance.

In any event, somehow after the brush with the police and Dallas, Roger made his way to Las Vegas. It was while he was in Las Vegas on Saturday, April 26, that Roger married a woman named Jennifer Ann Manning.

The honeymoon was short. The next day, Jennifer returned to San Diego.

Later, Jennifer would come to play a key role in the unfolding events surrounding the Doris Angleton murder—at least, a key role if the eventual police theory of the case is to be believed.

But at the time of the marriage, no one in Houston even knew who Jennifer was, let alone that she had just married a man suspected of murder, a man who had just told her that she was to be the beneficiary of a three-million-dollar life-insurance policy.

In the meantime, Bob returned to the homicide division, and, sitting with Ferguson at a computer terminal, they jointly composed two written statements; before signing them, he asked to take them home so he could go over them with George Tyson to make sure they were accurate, since they had to be signed under penalty of perjury. Ferguson said that would be fine. The statement about Roger was signed by Bob on May 2. In this statement, Roger elaborated on his past difficulties with Roger.

In addition to recounting the 1991 attack/extortion attempt, the agreement, and the March scene at Denny's, Bob provided copies of letters he'd received from Roger in 1990 that seemed to support his account of the differences he'd had with Roger. Bob also provided the detectives with a tape of the barely decipherable conversation between Doris and Roger, as well as photos of the bullet holes in the condo walls. Bob also cited a number of other people who were aware of the bad blood between the Angleton brothers.

After Roger moved to San Diego, Bob said, he and Doris wanted to be sure that Roger really was in California, and what he was up to. At Templeton's suggestion, Bob hired a private investigator, J. J. Gradoni, a former Houston police officer. Gradoni tracked Roger down in San Diego, and located a number of maildrops used by Roger.

''Gradoni's opinion was that Roger was very well

versed in covering his tracks," Bob said in his statement.

In the other statement, signed by Bob on April 28, Bob retraced his movements on the night of Doris' murder. The most critical question was the matter of Doris' movements, and the issue of Ali's bat—the one that had been left behind when Bob went first to the softball game.

"At approximately 7:15 P.M.," Bob wrote, "my wife Doris and my daughters arrived at the park while I was in the batting cage.

"My wife stopped her blue Suburban in the middle of Auden Street and honked the horn. As I started walking up to the car, the girls started getting out of the car.

"Doris' window was down. Doris then said that she was going home to change. I then said to Doris that I had left one of Ali's bats on the deck and I asked her to pick up the bat when she returns. I told Doris to get Ali's bat because I realized that I had forgot it when we were having team batting practice in the batting cage.

"Doris told me okay and then drove away. Niki then commented that Mom was wearing the ugliest shirt that she had ever seen and had told her to go home and change it."

This was important. The question was, Why had Doris returned to the house? Was the bat left behind deliberately as the bait in a trap to get her into the rear part of the house, where she could be murdered? Was Doris deliberately dispatched to retrieve the bat, or was she going home primarily to change, as Bob suggested?

After discussion about the events of the softball game and the return of Bob, Niki, and Ali to the house after the game, Bob described how the police had discovered Doris' body.

"A short time later the police exited the house," Bob's statement read. "The male officer came up to me and in a solemn fashion said, 'Sir, what was the color of the shirt you last saw your wife wearing?' or, 'Sir, was the the shirt you last saw your wife in white?'

"The message was clear and my legs buckled and I then started crying. The officer then told me not to do this in front of my children. He kept holding me up. I then went somewhere around the circular drive and started rolling in the grass."

The day following the murder, Bob said, he and Tex Welsh went back to the house to see if anything was missing. Doris' jewelry seemed untouched, Bob said. Next, Bob noticed that the safe in his closet was open.

"The night before, an officer asked me if 'I normally leave the safe open' and I answered, 'No,'" Bob said. "The safe was empty. I had approximately $10,000 to $12,000 in the safe. I remember that when I left for my daughters' softball game the previous evening, the safe was closed because I had been in my closet to change into my coach's shirt. It is a combination safe. I have the combination and my wife has the combination. There is no one else I know of [who] has the combination."

The detectives considered this a significant amendment of Bob's initial remark about the safe on the night of the murder, when a police officer claimed that Bob told him that the safe was always kept open.

He and Tex found nothing else missing, Bob said in his statement.

"As I was coming down the front stairs with Tex," Bob added, "I made the comment to Tex, 'This wasn't a robbery,' meaning it wasn't a random burglary."

By early May, the Houston police had assembled enough information about Roger to justify going to California to see whether his trail could be picked up. Ferguson and Wright made the trip.

First the detectives went to Los Angeles, where they located Roger's first wife. From her they learned that Roger had been in very poor health over the last few years, primarily from a bad back, but also a weak heart. Roger had also become addicted to painkilling prescriptions, they learned. Roger's health had become so bad, his first wife said, she'd told him to move out because it was disrupting her life.

Ferguson and Wright now went to San Diego, where Roger's history went back to at least early 1989; county records indicated he registered the fictitious names of two businesses, GP Tract Services and San Diego Physical Therapy, on February 6, 1989. This, of course, was more than a year and a half before Bob had fired him from the Houston book.

In the wake of the pay-off by Bob, Roger returned

to San Diego, and started another new business, Auto Flex, in June of 1991. A little more than a year later, Roger returned to the real estate business by starting Limited Edition Homes, which he incorporated two years later.

It appeared that it was sometime during this period that Roger first met Jennifer Manning; records showed that Roger and Jennifer were co-owners of an enterprise named U.S. Homes as of July 1993.

Over the next two years, Roger formed two more businesses, Real Estate Services in August 1994, and American Century Properties in September of 1996.

Roger also had a minor criminal history in San Diego, having been arrested on May 1, 1991 for driving under the influence; he was placed on probation. Then, in October of 1996, Roger was arrested for illegally attempting to obtain prescription drugs. A trial date was set for April 16 the following year— as it turned out, the same day Doris was murdered. As a result of his failure to appear, a bench warrant for Roger had been issued by the San Diego court.

The Houston detectives asked their San Diego counterparts to notify them if anyone happened to pick up Roger on the warrant; obviously, they did not want Roger to be released until they had a chance to talk to him.

Unbeknownst to Ferguson and Wright, Bob was also looking for Roger. Three days after the murder, Bob had hired J. J. Gradoni once more to find Roger. He didn't believe that the Houston police were taking his story about Roger seriously, his lawyers said later, and didn't think they were doing anything to find

Roger, who, in Bob's view, was violently deranged. So he paid J. J. Gradoni $6,000 to do the job.

Gradoni had a man in San Diego who tracked down an address for Roger. Gradoni's man staked the house out, but Roger didn't show. Instead, a woman appeared to be living in the house. Gradoni's man informed Gradoni, who in turn informed the San Diego authorities that he had located an address for a man they wanted. The San Diego authorities notified Novak, who then called Gradoni; Novak then told Gradoni to tell his operative to back off.

In the meantime, Roger's house was also under surveillance by a deputy U.S. Marshal; just what the U.S. Marshal's office wanted with Roger was never made clear. But the deputy also told Gradoni's operative to beat it.

Meanwhile, Ferguson and Wright arrived at the house, which they soon discovered was occupied by Jennifer Ann Manning. At that time Ferguson and Novak had no idea who Jennifer Ann Manning was.

Ferguson and Novak soon discovered that Jennifer was in the real estate business with the missing Roger, as well as the fact that she and Roger had married just ten days after the murder.

Where was Roger? Wright and Ferguson asked Jennifer. Jennifer said she wasn't sure. She met with her new husband at the La Jolla Marriott hotel on May 1, and again in Santa Monica on May 9, but she didn't know where Roger was at that moment.

Ferguson and Wright were skeptical.

''I believe she knew where he was, but wouldn't

tell us," Ferguson said later. "We knew Jennifer knew where he was, there's no doubt in my mind that she knew. She just wasn't going to tell us."

Ferguson formed the impression that Roger and Jennifer had an unconventional marriage, particularly given Roger's apparent perambulations and Jennifer's seeming ignorance of his whereabouts.

"They had, I guess you could say, a bizarre relationship, Jennifer and Roger," Ferguson said. "They didn't have much of a sex life, according to Jennifer. But we felt like at the time that Jennifer knew more about this killing than she was telling us. And we felt like the only reason they got married was because of the wife-husband privilege."

But so far as Roger was concerned, San Diego seemed to be a dry hole. Ferguson and Wright returned to Houston.

SEVENTEEN

After San Diego, the investigation into Doris' murder settled into a sort of lull. Efforts were made to discern Roger's whereabouts by tracking his credit card expenditures, but these seemed suddenly to dry up; indeed, several accounts had maxed out or had been shut down for non-payment. One weird thing: Roger rented two cars in Houston on the day before Doris' murder, each from a different agency. Neither car had yet been returned.

One interesting lead did develop, however; Roger was evicted from the apartment he'd rented not far from Bob's courier service. When investigators searched the dwelling the day after Roger was evicted on April 24, they uncovered several interesting items: an IBM Selectric typewriter, missing its type element; and a crumpled-up piece of paper wedged under the machine.

The typewritten letter was an almost exact match to the wording in the note Bob said he'd gotten from Roger early in March.

Dear Bob,
   Although we parted ways in 1990 on very bad terms, your fault, I want to see you . . . it would be very important to you that we meet, if not it would be a big mistake on your part. Write me at [Roger's mailbox in San Diego] *and/or give me a telephone number I can call you at . . .*

Below this was another note:

dear bob,
   after seeing you, I GAVE THIS ALL SOME GREAT AMOUNT OF THOUGH[t] AND I DECIDED THAT MY POSITION WITH YOU IS FINAL AND NOT NEGOTIABLE. IF YOU DON'T GIVE ME $200,000.00 I PROMISE THAT I WILL HURT YOU IN A WAY THAT WILL BE WITH YOU THE REST OF YOUR LIFE . . . I HAVE NOTHING TO LOSE. I WILL GIVE YOU UNTIL LATE MARCH, IF I DON'T HEAR FROM YOU, I AM COMING THERE AND WILL MAKE YOU PAY. I WILL NOT MEET YOU ALONE, SO DON'T THINK OF ANY TRICKS, LIKE THE LAW 0R WHATEVER. THINK ABOUT THIS. AGAIN MY ADDRESS IS . . .

Other than those two items, the apartment was completely empty.

That prompted some thinking on the part of the detectives, and later the prosecutors: It almost seemed to the authorities that Roger was leaving a trail of bread crumbs to entice the police to come after him.

As McClellan, the prosecutor, put it later, "Now, you will find this is exactly the same language that appears in the handwritten note, and that is what I think is unique about the stuff that he turns over to Bob, is addressed to Bob, and is signed by Roger. Nothing else in this entire [case] is addressed to anybody, or signed by anybody. Those [are] things he knew would get to the police, so the police will know what to do, will have 'Dear Bob,' and 'from Roger.' "

In other words, according to McClellan, the two notes, one given to the police by Bob and the other found in Roger's rented apartment, lay down the scenario that Roger was out to injure Bob, and was the evil brother, while Bob was the innocent victim.

But to Ferguson and Novak at the time, and to McClellan and Wilson later, it seemed much too pat. Why, for example, was the typewritten note left in the apartment when everything else was cleaned out? It seemed that Roger was bent on giving Bob a scapegoat for Doris' murder.

But this tantalizing hint was barely digested when a sudden squall broke over the Houston Police Department on the subject of Bob's bookmaking operation and his relationship with the vice officer Templeton.

In a May 23 story headlined "Inquiry of Brutal Shooting Focuses on Husband's Dealings," the

Houston Chronicle's S. K. Bardwell spilled the beans on Bob's bookmaking, as well as the fact that he was an informant for the department. This was exactly what Bob and Templeton had feared would happen on the day after Doris' murder. The fact that the secret had kept as long as it had was remarkable.

"Police officials say the victim's husband, Robert Nicholas Angleton, 48, is involved in gambling and was used as an informant by HPD's vice division," Bardwell wrote.

A close reading of Bardwell's article, coupled with the fact that the information about Bob appeared to be coming from anonymous sources inside the police department, suggested a split between the homicide detectives and the vice division.

"The department has protected [Angleton] for nearly a decade, and his business has flourished," Bardwell quoted an unnamed police officer.

Bardwell sought a comment on the situation from Houston assistant chief Art Contreras, who was in charge of the vice division.

Calling the use of informants "a necessary evil," Contreras agreed that Bob had worked as an informant "for quite some time." But Bob wasn't paid for this work, Contreras added—an assertion that would later be disputed by lawyers for Bob.

Bob, meanwhile, was trying to pull his head down. He told Bardwell that any characterization of him as an informant was "more than likely incorrect. No such thing." And Bob denied that he was a bookmaker.

Next Bardwell tracked down two convicted book-

makers who claimed that Bob had set them up to be
arrested by Templeton, only to take over their customers later.

Bardwell called Templeton, but Templeton didn't
call back.

The unnamed officers rounded out Bardwell's exposé of Bob and Templeton, and again the depart-
mental split seemed apparent.

"Depending on who you ask, Bob Angleton is
booking $20 million to $40 million a year," one officer said. "The reason he's so successful, is he's put
so many other, smaller bookies out of business.
That's what's wrong with this picture: By using a
handful of guys like Angleton to bust the rest of the
bookies, the police department isn't stopping or re-
ducing gambling." Instead, all the department was
doing was consolidating the vice into one person's
control, making that one person rich.

A vice officer disagreed with this, however. "It
does more than that. It helps us control the activity.
We know who's doing what, and we keep them in
line."

But the officer who was critical of the arrangement
disagreed.

"In other places, the Mafia does that," the officer
shot back. "That's not what we're supposed to do."

Bob's unmasking as a bookmaker and putative informant set the River Oaks tongues atwitter. All of a
sudden, it appeared that many people had known of
Bob's bookmaking, even when they really didn't.
Later, *Texas Monthly*'s Hollandsworth was to encounter a River Oaks woman who had asked her

friend Doris just what it was that Bob did for a living.

"He's a bookmaker," Doris said matter-of-factly.

"Why, I had no idea he was so literary," the woman told Doris.

Others now recalled Bob at the Briar Club, swimming laps in the pool, pausing at the end of each lap to talk on his cellular telephone, apparently taking and placing bets. Some of the board members of the club had become convinced that Bob was using the club for his bookmaking activities, and an informal discussion was held about whether to throw Bob out of the club. In the end, probably because of Doris, nothing was done, however.

Shortly after the *Chronicle*'s exposé was published, Bob encountered one of Doris' friends, one of the softball mothers, and a Briar Club member.

Wasn't Bob worried that he'd be arrested for bookmaking? the woman asked. Who would take care of the girls if that happened?

He didn't think he'd be arrested for bookmaking, Bob replied. If he was arrested, he continued, it would be for something a lot worse than that.

What's that? the woman asked, fascinated.

Capital murder, Bob replied; it had not gone unnoticed by Bob that the Houston homicide cops were skeptical of his my-big-brother-did-it story.

FINDING ROGER

EIGHTEEN

Big brother was starting to fade, however.

By June 22, 1997, Roger was in Las Vegas, and worn out from all the moving around. He arrived at the Alexis Park Hotel and tried to check in, paying cash, about 9:30 P.M.

When desk clerk Shani Coleman asked Roger for some identification, Roger produced a Texas driver's license in the name of Lee Peter Glenn, with a Houston address.

Going to the copy machine, Coleman noticed something odd about the license: The lower portion showing the driver's name was on a piece of paper folded over and fixed to the back of the license. Coleman unfolded the paper and saw another name, the one the license had actually been issued to: Roger Nicholas Angleton of El Paso.

Unaware that Coleman suspected something was amiss, Roger checked into his room. But Coleman, meanwhile, called the Las Vegas police and reported that someone had just checked in with a phony driver's license.

Two Las Vegas police officers arrived and demanded admittance to Roger's room. By that time they had checked with the criminal warrant computer system and knew that Roger was wanted for attempted drug possession in San Diego. They arrested Roger.

What happened next would have been highly controversial if not for subsequent events. The officers later said they asked Roger for permission to search the room; apparently, they believed that it was likely that Roger had illegal drugs.

The Las Vegas officers later said that Roger had given them permission to search. But in the absence of a signed waiver, that was later to seem highly unlikely, even to the Houston prosecutors.

In any event, the two Las Vegas police officers first searched Roger, and almost immediately discovered $64,282 in cash; the money was wrapped in tape in small stacks and stapled together, so ''that the money could be concealed from a body search,'' as the Las Vegas police put it.

Underneath a sofa, the searchers discovered a briefcase. Opening it, the police found a number of papers, envelopes, a book about disguises, several bottles of painkillers, and a blue folder filled with various handwritten and typewritten notes. The officers seized the cash, the briefcase, the folder, Roger's luggage, and Roger himself.

Despite the Houston investigators' request that San Diego notify them as soon as Roger resurfaced, something went awry. The word went from Las Vegas to San Diego that the man wanted on the San Diego bench warrant had been apprehended, but someone on the San Diego end apparently didn't feel Roger was worth extracting from Las Vegas, since the San Diego drug charge was only a misdemeanor. But no one notified Houston that Roger was now available.

What happened next was somewhat confusing; the Houston authorities never really sorted out the actual sequence of events. But apparently Roger, while in jail, began suffering from ever more serious health problems. Soon he was transferred to a hospital, where he underwent some sort of surgery. The bill for the medical treatment, Houston officials said they were later told, ran more than $40,000. But almost as soon as Roger recovered, he tried to escape from the hospital. Now Roger was under arrest for this, as well, and was soon back in the Clark County jail.

Still no one in Houston was aware of Roger's whereabouts, and wouldn't be until well into the next month.

On July 10, Jennifer Manning checked into the Holiday Inn in Houston. Jennifer then took a taxi to Roadrunner Couriers, Bob's business. The way the police pieced the story together later, Jennifer walked into the office and asked for George Davidson.

As it happened, George Davidson was the former owner of Roadrunner Couriers, and had been bought out by Bob over a period of time in the early 1990s; he had been one of the go-betweens for Roger and Bob in the 1991 dispute. What Roger apparently did not know, however, was that George Davidson had died several years earlier in a car wreck.

When Jennifer was told that George was dead, she seemed flustered and unsure of what to do next. She left, went to a telephone, and somehow reached Roger in jail.

George Davidson is dead, Jennifer told Roger.

Roger told Jennifer to go back to Roadrunner and ask for Bob. When she was told Bob wasn't in, Jennifer left an envelope for him.

With that, Jennifer returned to the Holiday Inn to wait for Bob to come to her.

In fact, Bob was out of town over the weekend, and moreover, was about to leave with Niki and Ali for a vacation in Hawaii. He did not learn of the letter from Jennifer until Monday. Opening it, Bob read, "My name is Jennifer Manning Angleton, in Room 713 at the Holiday Inn. Life and Death. Come immediately."

But because it was now Monday, it was too late. Jennifer Ann Manning Angleton had already checked out of the hotel.

Bob now called Ferguson. Ferguson wasn't available, so Bob left a message on Ferguson's voice mail.

"When I came into work Wednesday, I had a message from Bob saying he had received a letter from, he thinks, Roger, trying to contact him," Ferguson said later. "The letter was addressed to someone with a Greek name, and it had a couple of numbers. So I try to get hold of Bob, and I find out he's enroute to Dallas with his kids, they're going to Los Angeles and Hawaii."

Ferguson called Bob back, and learned that he'd

given the letter to Tyson. Novak picked up the letter, and learned that it had been delivered to Roadrunner by Jennifer.

This naturally piqued the detectives' interest in Jennifer; if she was trying to contact Bob, was it likely that she knew where Roger was hiding? Ferguson thought the chances were excellent. In fact, it was beginning to look like Jennifer was the cut-out between Bob and Roger—if you believed that Roger and Bob were in on Doris' murder together, as Ferguson had not yet dismissed as a distinct possibility.

Ferguson asked his department's crime analysis unit to obtain copies of Jennifer's long-distance call records. After a few days, the records were delivered. All the records showed were the numbers dialed and the length of the call.

Methodically calling each of the numbers one by one to see who answered, Ferguson was rewarded at last:

"Clark County jail," came the answer.

"I was surprised as heck, so I just hung up," Ferguson said later. "I said, that S.O.B. is in jail. I called the Las Vegas police. Do you-all have Roger Angleton in jail? Yes we do. When was he arrested? June 22. I said, son of a gun.

"So things kind of went from there. The detention center put me in touch with Las Vegas detectives, who gave me a rundown on the arrest, the hotel room, the briefcase, and what was in the briefcase." The startling information that Roger had more than $64,000 with him when he was arrested tended to firm up Ferguson's suspicion that Bob was involved

in his wife's murder. Where would Roger get that
kind of money, if not from Bob? It wasn't like Roger
was doing a lot of real estate deals while he was on
the lam.

NINETEEN

By the Wednesday of the following week, Ferguson
and Novak were on their way to Las Vegas to interview Roger and to inspect the contents of the briefcase, the folder, and Roger's luggage.

Flying to Las Vegas, Novak remembered the microcasette recorder that had been found in the suitcase at the Dallas-Fort Worth airport. Novak made a
joke: Wouldn't it be something if the briefcase had a
microcasette tape in it? After all, it seemed the brothers had a penchant for surreptitiously taping each
other, as the Denny's frisking incident suggested.

That would be very funny, Ferguson agreed.

Apart from noticing Roger's painkillers and the cash,
the Las Vegas police hadn't paid much attention to
the contents of the briefcase, or the blue folder, for
that matter. But Ferguson and Novak wanted to be
cautious; before leaving, they obtained a court order
from Houston Judge Ted Poe authorizing them to
take possession of the briefcase, the cash, and the
folder.

They went over the briefcase first, and very carefully.

"We put our gloves on," Ferguson recalled. "We started seeing these notes about, what looked like to us, things to do, what days Doris was doing what. It had what looked like a contract . . ."

Ferguson and Novak had struck a deep gusher of potentially vital evidence.

For openers, there was a lined piece of paper that looked very similar to the handwritten notes on Doris' schedule found in the Dallas-Fort Worth airport suitcase.

Apparently headed "4-9," along the left-hand margin were a series of numbers, followed by zeros or asterisks, then a day of the week, followed by notations that were at once cryptic and difficult to read:

> 9 0 Wed Mother Ni10 pm
> 10 * Thur 7:45 game (gone to game) (indecipherable)/ Big kids
> 11 0 Fri Ruggles birthday
> 12 0 Possible (indecipherable) 12-10-49 (indecipherable)
> 13 Sun Birthday 0 5:00 pm (indecipherable) Photo Houston
> 14 * Mon practice 8:00–9:15 (indecipherable)
> 16 * W Game 7:45
> 0 Notes in calendar (indecipherable) 9 pm
> 21 M Game   6 pm
> 24 * Thurs Game 7:45
> -civnnat
> after 24th 90 for hit
> (indecipherable) / Smith (indecipherable)

Then, down in the right-hand corner under the heading "1/30383" were three words:

Grottos   46
Carrabbas   47
Cafe Express   48

The top of the page held still more cryptic notes, containing numbers and words, such as "6971132 go," "1 1-11 study ckns," "11-11-16 main gr," and over on the right-hand side, "8184*," "00032," "Power," a word that could be "night," followed by "= get out."

By this time, Novak and Ferguson were fairly familiar with Doris' April schedule and her habits. The numbers on the left margin were certainly dates, followed by the girls' softball schedule; most intriguing was the fact that the schedule appeared to go beyond April 16, the night Doris was shot.

If Roger had been stalking Doris, how would he know where she was supposed to be after she was dead? The fact that games were scheduled for April 21 and April 24 surely indicated that Roger had some sort of inside information about Doris' future whereabouts, as did the notation, "notes in calendar," which implied that Roger had access to Doris' personal calendar. The list in the right-hand corner, "Grottos," "Carrabbas," and "Cafe Express," were restaurants favored by Doris.

The top of the page was also interesting. In his statement to the police, Bob had provided his electric gate code, "8184," and the alarm code to the house,

"00032." Now here they were, along with some other numbers that might be significant to Bob.

The note at the bottom was chilling: "After 24th, 90 for hit."

Did this mean that the price for Doris' murder would go down if it took place after April 24?

And finally, the fact that each day with an asterisk was also the day of a softball game or practice seemed significant—each day marked a time that Doris might be alone at the Ella Lee address for at least a short period of time.

But there was a lot more in Roger's briefcase, as it turned out.

As they continued sifting through the papers, Ferguson and Novak soon came across three typewritten documents; it appeared that each had been typed on the same machine used for the threatening note found in Roger's one-month Houston apartment.

One appeared to be a set of instructions:

ENTER ABOUT 8:15-30 via gate and side door
disarm system 00032 (possible re-arm) gate code * or
*   #8184*
Let dog out.
wait in kitchen [handwritten, indecipherable]
subject comes home, hit immediately if with either girl
*   leave via back entrance*
rummage house plus watch prob no ring unless off in
*   dish in bathroom*
leave via back entrance, tape and break window for
*   entrance, leave door open*
leave gate open or leave sign in front of house that this
*   is done.*

(can page you with code that is done)

---

if paged 1111 or whatever abort or telephone 1/2-1/2-
? safe ?
can leave front door, leave open
if abort, how get dog back in, steak
pointof hit to leave 3 minutes
if not going to game, page signal
preference thursday or following or following Wednes-
    day
Monday possible if you can get her temporarily out of
    the house . . .
Galveston has problems, where put car, arrives with
    girlfriend or girlfriend comes to soon

Clearly, these were instructions using information from someone intimately familiar with the Ella Lee house. The fact that the entry codes were known, that a dog was present, that there was a possibility of a ring in a soapdish in the bathroom, that a game was involved, and that "Galveston"—the beach house—"has problems," all indicated that someone had access to information about the Angletons.

Then there was the phrase "leave sign in front of house that this is done," indicating that someone would be arriving after the deed who wanted advance warning of what could be expected. Who would that be? The most logical person who would want such warning was Bob.

Next there was what appeared to be a contract:

money 125,000
October 20 or so 100,000 and 1000, 000 thereafter an-

nualized in October until 2005 (less 12,000 advanced
vanced
if arrested keep paying to designee.
on future money have to work with me as to when and
where
have to know[n] whether you delvier [sic] letters that
night or not
will send future vendetta letter which will clinch

MY CONTRACT WITH YOU IS THE KILL AND NO SQUEELING [sic], IF KILLED CUT MONEY TO DESIGNATED PARTIES. THE METHOD DESIGNED BY ME IS TO GIVE YOU ALIBI AND PERMIT POLICE TO FOCUS ON ME.

MONEY LEAVE NOTE AT PHARMACY AS TO WHERE,
[G]IVE ME MAILBOX KEY AND NUMBER AND I
will leave letters

This seemed entirely plain: Someone was offering to take the blame for "the kill and no squeeling." In return, that someone was asking for varying amounts of money—$125,000, $100,000, and "1000, 000" (either $100,000 or $1,000,000, depending on the typist's intent) every year until 2005, less, of course, the "12,000" advanced.

Also implicit in this apparent bargain was a method of future contact: "MONEY LEAVE NOTE AT PHARMACY AS TO WHERE." As it happened, Bob owned a small shopping center that included a pharmacy not far from the Ella Lee house.

The next typewritten document appeared to be in-

structions on how someone should act if questioned
by the police:

POLICE:
WHEN, WHERE WHY DID SEE BROTHER LAST
    OR COMMUNICATE WITH HIM
WILL GIVE YOU CHRONOLOGY COORDINATED
    WITH LETTERS
YOUR ATTITUDE WHEN YOU RELEASE LET-
    TERS IS THAT ROGER WAS DESPERATE, AN-
    GRREY [sic] AND BROKE [sic] ON DRUGS AND
    ALCOHOL. ATTEMPTED BLACKMAIL AND/
    OR THREATS. DIDN'T TAKE SERIOUSLY BE-
    CAUSE INCOMPASITATED. [sic]
PURCHASED KILL GUN IN MY NAME
IF POLICE INFER OR ASK ANY QUESTIONS
    WHICH ARE TOO DETAILED OR LEADING TO
    YOU AS INVOLVED CUT THEM OFF IN AN-
    GER AND HIRE DETECTIVES TO FIND ME.

Well, wasn't this exactly what Bob had been telling the police ever since April 17? That "Roger"
was desperate and angry, that he seemed worn out,
on drugs and alcohol? Hadn't Bob hired J. J. Gradoni
to find Roger?

And what about the "letters"? There had been two
so far: the March 7 note, in which Roger had sworn
to make Bob "pay dearly," and the summons to the
Holiday Inn meeting with Jennifer Manning on a
matter of "life and death." And what was all this in
the supposed contract about "will send future vendetta letter to clinch"?

In the documents found in Las Vegas, Ferguson
and Novak unearthed two pages of what appeared to

be Roger's scrawled handwriting, one on a blank piece of paper, the other on the same sort of lined theme book paper used in the March 7 note to Bob.

Roger's handwriting was never up to Parker methods, but these were worse than ever.

One appeared to be titled, "Elements of Letters." It read:

I made good on my threat. Doris is gone. But you should have kept this between you and me. I suspect police involvement & watching home. [indecipherable] Probably tapping phones or maybe they're just detective or bounty hunter.

Look, if cops involved do what you have to call them off—otherwise [indecipherable] I and my friend will take out your daughters. He can hit a half-dollar at 300 yards.

There was more, but Roger's handwriting severely deteriorated at that point, almost into incomprehensibility.

The same was true with the second handwritten note, the one on the lined paper. This one contained a legible reference to "auto weapon," followed by a directive, "call them off, I don't care how you do it, if you don't your spoiled brat daughters are history also."

It continued, "Keep this between us. Doris is gone but you keep up [indecipherable]. So will your kids."

This was signed, "Fuck you, R."

These two scrawled documents appeared, at least

to the detectives, to be drafts of the "vendetta letters" referred to in the contract. The most interesting thing in the drafts, however, was the reference to "my friend . . . [who] . . . can hit a half-dollar at 300 yards." This seemed to indicate that Roger was preparing to tell Bob that he had an expert marksman as an accomplice.

As far as Ferguson and Novak knew, however, Bob had received no such letters from Roger; if he had, he certainly hadn't yet provided them to the police.

Finally, there was a substantial amount of material relating to spousal privilege—what a husband or wife can or cannot say if called to testify. That, to Ferguson and Novak, meant only one thing: Roger had drilled Jennifer Manning as to what her rights were. In addition, there were two passports in the briefcase: one for Roger Angleton, and the other for Jennifer Ann Manning.

On the surface, there were two ways to take all this material.

First, this was evidence of a murder contract between Roger and Bob, in which Roger agreed to take the blame for murdering Doris in return for a substantial amount of money.

Or alternatively, it might be evidence of Roger's intent to extort Bob—even by going so far as to fabricate documents that appeared to indicate, however falsely, that Bob was involved in the plot.

"And then we found a little microcasette," Ferguson said later.

TWENTY

Almost as soon as Ferguson and Novak discovered the microcasette, they recalled the joke they had shared on the plane to Las Vegas.

Was it possible there was something on the tape that might shed light on Doris' murder? After all, an empty microcasette recorder had been recovered in the suitcase at the Dallas-Fort Worth airport.

Because of the potential legal problems with Roger's search by the Las Vegas police, it was decided to obtain a search warrant for the tape from a Houston judge. First, however, Novak and Ferguson held an interview with Roger.

Just what Roger told the detectives at this point was never made public, for a variety of reasons. It does seem fairly clear, however, that Roger made no admissions concerning Doris' murder or his brother's possible involvement. What the detectives took away from their discussion with Roger, however, was an appreciation for the tone of Roger's voice, his pace of speaking, and the way he formed his words. Having interviewed Bob and listened to various tapes of Bob's voice, the detectives were struck by how similar the two brothers sounded.

But before the detectives attempted to listen to the tape, even with a search warrant, they had some unfinished business with Jennifer Manning. On July 25, they flew to San Diego to reinterview Jennifer.

*   *   *

The question was, What had Jennifer been up to when she'd come to Houston to see Bob?

The interview was apparently conducted over the telephone, according to court documents later filed in the case against Roger and Bob.

As Ferguson later told it, Jennifer said she'd first called Roger in the Las Vegas jail early in June, and had then gone to visit him about July 5. There Roger had given her some instructions: She was to go to Roadrunner, ask for Davidson, and drop off the envelope with the Greek name on it, making certain that Davidson knew it was "a matter of life or death." Then she was to go back to the hotel and wait for Bob to show up; whereupon she was to give Bob another envelope. But Bob never showed.

What was in this letter she was supposed to give Bob?

Jennifer told the detectives that she didn't know, only that she was supposed to give it to Bob in the hotel room.

The following day, Ferguson and Novak returned to Las Vegas, still not satisfied that Jennifer was telling everything she knew. Indeed, they remained convinced that Jennifer had much more to say, particularly after Jennifer told them she was going to Las Vegas to visit Roger.

What Ferguson and Novak had not discovered from Jennifer was the fact that she did indeed know the contents of the envelope from Roger to Bob, and that even as the detectives were interviewing her, Jennifer

was in the midst of a new attempt by Roger to contact
Bob. All of this was to come out later—much later—
as the case against Bob neared trial.

As Ferguson and McClellan described the story
later, Jennifer's efforts to establish communication
between her new husband and Bob began early in
July, when she visited Roger in the Clark County jail.

Holding a piece of paper with a written message
to the glass between them in the visiting area, Roger
had Jennifer copy the words he wanted to deliver to
Bob. Jennifer later typed the words in a letter, which
she then placed inside the envelope she intended to
give Bob in the Holiday Inn on July 11.

Ferguson later paraphrased the contents of this
note.

"Basically, it was, please give bearer $85,000 fast.
Says he can't get to his money. Had a heart attack.
Says he's just out of surgery. Says he was arrested,
might get out with right attorney. Charges are bogus.
Have been questioned. Gave no answers. Says [will
not] implicate others. Told there's no chance to deal.
Do not talk to police anymore. They are devious and
trouble, but in the end have zero. And says please
give bearer of this note $100,000 per year for eight
years starting in January 1998."

This was language that, in Ferguson's view, was
highly suggestive of a conspiracy between Roger and
his brother. "Have been questioned. Gave no answers. Will not implicate others."

Or, alternatively: Was this a threat by Roger to
falsely implicate Bob in Doris' murder? A threat that,

if Bob didn't pay up, Roger *would* "implicate others"?

The trouble was, neither the detectives nor Bob knew about this note, because Bob had not been able to collect it on July 11, and because Jennifer did not tell Novak and Ferguson that she knew its contents when they interviewed her on July 25.

Nor did Jennifer tell Novak and Ferguson that at some point after leaving Houston she'd gone back to Las Vegas, visited Roger in jail again, and obtained new instructions for Bob.

"And then Roger started giving her details as to what to typewrite in the second letter," Ferguson said he and Novak learned later. "This was a letter that was a lot more detailed, a one-page, typewritten, single-spaced letter. She gets the information, writes all this stuff down that Roger told her to type in this letter. She gets all the information, goes back to San Diego, then she types out this letter.

"And Roger had also told her, go open a post office box, and mail these letters to Bob. At Roadrunner. She opens up a post office box in Monarch Beach, California. She then mails those two letters— the little short one I just told you about—and the long one by overnight mail. Anyway, they're delivered to Roadrunner. Roadrunner gets them, Tex gets them, opens them up, sees what they are, and apparently contacts Bob, and Bob's already in Hawaii."

The long letter, according to Ferguson and McClellan, was the most explicit yet between Roger and Bob.

In this letter, Roger told Bob that because of the

new circumstances—presumably, that he'd now been jailed and that Bob hadn't responded to Jennifer's plea to meet him at the Holiday Inn—he and Bob were going to have to change their arrangements, that payments were going to have to be made a different way; at one point in the long letter, Roger told Bob that he was still committed to their supposed bargain, and as McClellan recalled it, "up to and including suicide."

"Basically it's a communication from a person who has made a deal with someone to a person who has promised them something to say [I did it]," McClellan said. "That communication is not signed, there's nothing that says, now, here it is, this is Roger talking."

At this point Tex told Bob what had just been delivered at the courier service.

"Bob asks Tex to fax them to him," Ferguson said. "So then Tex sent faxes of the letters to Hawaii, Lahaina," where Bob and the girls were having their vacation at the Royal Lahaina Hotel.

After receiving the faxes, Bob composed two notes to send back to Jennifer at the Monarch Beach post office box.

In the first note, sent on July 22, Bob wrote that mail sent to Roadrunner would be forwarded to the police; in the second note, mailed the following day, Bob posed some hypothetical questions to be forwarded by Jennifer to Roger, suggesting that Roger explain just what he, Bob, should do if the police tried to implicate him, and putting forward the notion that the brothers should "resolve what ifs" before anything was decided.

These were both equivocal messages that could be read as either conspiratorial or an effort to develop evidence against Roger.

Ferguson, however, later came to believe that Bob was trying to "give her some little message, to get Roger to back off. Be cool. And the second one is, 'resolve what ifs,' I guess, what if the police try to bring me into this again, what's the next plan? That's my opinion."

But Jennifer's reticence in her interview of July 25 deprived the detectives of any knowledge of any of these communications, whether sinister or benign; as for his part, Bob did not immediately disclose them, either.

After a week in Lahaina, Bob and the girls returned to Houston late on July 28 or early on July 29. Whether Bob would have voluntarily disclosed these communications with Roger via Jennifer can't be determined, because matters were moving rapidly forward in another area.

TWENTY-ONE

After picking up Roger's ill-fated briefcase during their stopover in Las Vegas, Ferguson and Novak returned to Houston, obtained the search warrant for the tape, and sat down with prosecutor Ted Wilson to listen to it, even as Bob and the girls were returning from Hawaii.

The tape was about forty minutes long, and extraordinarily difficult to listen to. It was almost immediately clear to Ferguson and Novak that it had probably been surreptitiously recorded, because numerous parts of the conversation were muffled and indistinct, and the noise of the tape drive nearly drowned out the voices, indicating that the gain on the microphone had been turned up very high.

Based on remarks made on the tape, Ferguson and Novak later came to believe that the tape had been made on April 14, just two days before Doris was murdered.

It was also almost instantly clear to Ferguson and Novak—although, as it would turn out, not to others—that the two men talking on the tape were none other than Roger and Bob themselves.

Both voices displayed a nearly identical, almost adenoidal tonality, a medium to high timbre, along with a fast pace of talking that marked the speakers as not native Texans, but rather people from the East Coast. The fact that the voices spoke over one another clearly showed there were two men, not one playing two different roles.

Because the two men sounded so much alike, it was at first difficult to tell who was speaking. As the words became more clear, however, a difference in verbal demeanor began to emerge.

Eventually the tape was given to a special lab in the Houston Police Department, where an officer trained in such skills was able to enhance its quality. Still later, police attempted to transcribe the tape into written words; the written words were then transferred to a CD-ROM disc, which in turn was converted into a videotape, with the written words synchronized to the sounds. The police later declined to release their version of this written transcript, even though the videotape was entered into evidence against Bob.

Even with the police enhancement, there were numerous portions that remained unintelligible to the ordinary listener, and even what appeared to be some police errors in their transcription. With two men speaking so fast, and over each other, often turning away from the microphone, it was a long way from a high-fidelity recording. What follows here is a transcription of an audio tape made of the videotape that was entered into evidence.

The tape began with what sounded like a door closing, and the words of a man later labeled Voice Number One, who Ferguson and Novak believed was Roger Angleton, talking to a man labeled Voice Number Two, who they thought was Bob:

V2: Whew!
V1: Well, today's the day.
V2: Huh?
V1: Today's the day. The fourteenth.
V2: What?
V1: Today's the day.

The voice believed to be Roger's made some unintelligible comment.

V2: Hey, look. Want to [know?] about the burglar alarm? Read that.

It appeared that someone was showing a manual for the operation of the burglar alarm control system.

V2: It's not a white box. It's a black box.
V1: How's the daughter?
V2: It looks like she's going to make it.
V1: What was wrong, the flu?

The second voice made a comment about the daughter returning to school, then returned to the subject of the alarm system.

V2: Don't forget, the white box, not the black box. Don't try the white.
V1: All right.

One of the voices referred to a garage door opener. At almost the same time, it appeared that Voice Number One had produced some sort of list.

V1: I know what that is.
V2: That's a real dangerous list you've got there.
V1: I know. I know the risk. I just, when you'll go through it, I'll destroy it.
V2: Real dangerous. You're risking your neck to have it.
V1: I did that last night before I went to sleep.

After some more unintelligible comments, the discussion returned to the alarm system, as Voice Number Two kept trying to instruct Voice Number One on the operation of the alarm system, and what to expect.

Voice Number One next suggested an alternative method of dealing with a dog expected to be present, only to draw some exasperation from Voice Number Two.

V2: I thought we decided not to do it like that. I thought you decided that you're gonna put her in her little cage. That way if something blows like it did last time, then you're not—you're—

V1: Well, after the alarm—Okay. After the alarm—oh, in case someone comes along and sees or something?

V2: Or anything. You decided not to put her in there.

V1: I've got it, okay.

V2: Right?

V1: All right, I'll put her in the cage.

V2: Or put her in her washroom. [That's where she stays?] Just put her in the washroom. She'll [open?] the door.

After some more barely intelligible discussion, the speakers turned to the subject of a diamond ring, apparently an item on the list brought by Voice Number One.

V2: I don't like it. No cutting fingers off.

V1: You said go for the diamond.

The driveway of the Angleton home in River Oaks, Houston. Robert Angleton drove his Chevrolet Blazer into this carport, noticed that the side door, left, was open, and immediately backed the vehicle out to call 911. HARRIS COUNTY DISTRICT ATTORNEY'S OFFICE, EXHIBIT AT THE TRIAL OF ROBERT ANGLETON.

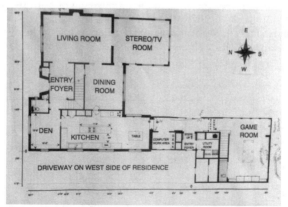

Crime scene diagram of the murder of Doris Angleton. Police investigators believed that Roger Angleton entered the Angleton residence via the driveway-side door, then waited until Doris arrived home to kill her in fulfillment of a contract with his brother Robert, Doris' husband. Doris' body was found dead between the hallway and the kitchen. HARRIS COUNTY DISTRICT ATTORNEY'S OFFICE, EXHIBIT IN THE TRIAL OF ROBERT ANGLETON.

The body of Doris Angleton, found on the night of April 16, 1997, in the family home in River Oaks. Doris sustained multiple gunshot wounds. Later, controversy would develop as to how many people shot her, and from which direction. HARRIS COUNTY DISTRICT ATTORNEY'S OFFICE, EXHIBIT IN THE TRIAL OF ROBERT ANGLETON.

Roger Angleton, brother of Robert Angleton. Roger, six years older than Robert, was accused of being the man who shot Doris 13 times on the night of April 16, 1997, to fulfill an alleged contract with his brother Robert. HARRIS COUNTY DISTRICT ATTORNEY'S OFFICE, EXHIBIT IN THE TRIAL OF ROBERT ANGLETON.

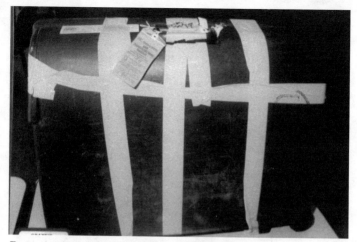

Roger Angleton's battered suitcase. Seized at the Dallas-Fort Worth airport in April, 1997, the contents of the suitcase helped Houston police link Roger Angleton to the murder of Doris. HARRIS COUNTY DISTRICT ATTORNEY'S OFFICE, EXHIBIT IN THE TRIAL OF ROBERT ANGLETON.

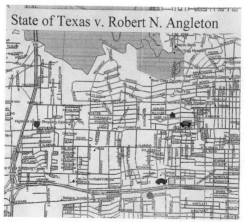

Map of West Loop, Houston, Texas. Locations of several events related to the murder of Doris Angleton. On the far left is the location of an apartment rented by Roger Angleton from late March to late April, 1997; the Angleton house is located in the upper-right quadrant. Also noted on the map are the recovery locations of two cars rented by Roger Angleton on the day before the murder. HARRIS COUNTY DISTRICT ATTORNEY'S OFFICE, EXHIBIT IN THE TRIAL OF ROBERT ANGLETON.

Sgt. David Ferguson, veteran Houston Police Department Homicide Detective. Ferguson and three other Houston detectives worked on the Angleton case for four months, and eventually arrested Robert and Roger Angleton for the premeditated murder of Doris Angleton.

Harris County Assistant District Attorney Ted Wilson. A veteran of the district attorney's special prosecutions section, Wilson was intimately familiar with gambling and organized crime in the Houston area.

Alessandra Angleton, 14, leaving the courtroom after her father's defense rested. *HOUSTON CHRONICLE*, STEVE CAMPBELL.

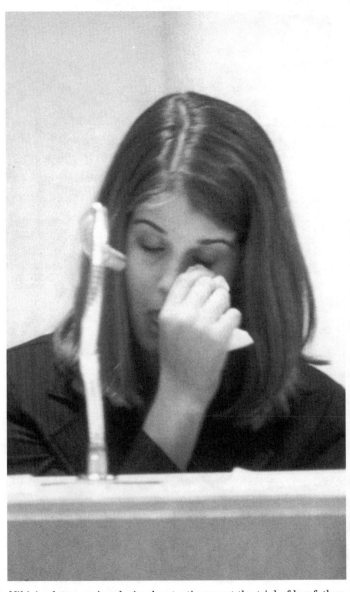

Niki Angleton crying during her testimony at the trial of her father.
Houston Chronicle, Steve Campbell.

Bob Angleton hugs one of his lawyers, Stan Schneider, when his acquittal is announced. *Houston Chronicle*, Ben DeSoto.

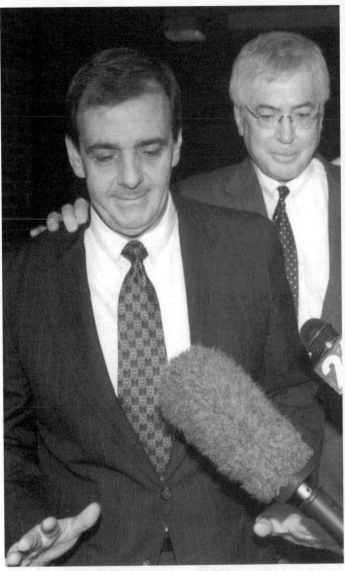

Accompanied by his lawyer, Mike Ramsey, Bob leaves the Harris County Jail following his acquittal. Angleton had been in jail for a little over a year. *HOUSTON CHRONICLE*, BEN DESOTO.

V2: I didn't say cut off the fucking finger to take the diamond.

V1: All right.

V2: I don't care for that.

V1: I didn't know what your reason was, I didn't ask.

V2: I don't want you cutting fingers.

V1: No, I wasn't gonna—

V2: If the thing doesn't slide right off—

V1: I was going to clip 'em. I was gonna clip 'em, all right?

Voice Number Two said something, apparently another objection to cutting fingers off.

V1: I don't care. If I clip 'em—

V2: [It has to look like] a person who was caught in the act.

V1: Yeah. And that's where actually none of this stuff will happen to me since I've panicked and left. Boom.

V2: Is the house rummaged?

V1: Yeah, that'll be happening. No. If I pre-rummage the house, see, that's the bitch. If I pre-rummage the house and something goes wrong, like if one of the girls come home—

V2: They're not going to know it was pre-rummaged, though.

An exchange over the issue of tossing the house to make it look like an interrupted burglary now took

place. Then Voice Number Two tried to get Voice
Number One to visualize the sequence of events, and
when it would be safe to fake the apparent burglary.

V2: You're waiting. She comes in, right?

V1: Yes.

V2: You hit her. Then you can rummage the
house.

V1: Right.

V2: There's nothing wrong with—

V1: No, no, I understand. I thought you said, *pre-
rummage* the house.

V2: No.

V1: No. But like you just said, the guy is
caught up, you're panicked, and he rum-
mages the house and left, he just happens
to—

V2: Yeah. But then, what I'm saying is, you
know, okay . . . no, rummage the house. By
cutting the ring off—you happen to have
caught her by surprise, right? She's caught
you by surprise. You shoot her, you go, oh
shit, you're out [the door].

V1: Oh, yeah, right, okay. But if it's in their focus . . . you know what I'm saying, it might—

V2: Tell them where to go.

After more discussion of movement around the
house, and various doors, the conversation turned to
more questions from Voice Number One.

V1: Now, do I lock the other door?

V2: Why?

V1: Wouldn't a normal, half-assed burglar attempt the other door, before he broke into that one, the one around the garage? The one around your office?

Voice Number Two did not directly respond to this, but read a checklist of movements, concluding with leaving the back door open, which Voice Number One thought would look funny, or possibly, breaking a window and leaving it with tape around the broken glass.

V1: Now you're going in the driveway and you're going to see the tape and halt.

V2: Something like that.

V1: And if for some reason, if things happen, if for some reason, I don't do the tape, I'll call for reference, a red piece of paper, and then you'll drive up in the driveway, before you get to to your gate, you'll see a red, right there.

V2: All right.

V1: Now—

V2: That means I have to go in myself.

V1: Right.

Now there was a considerable amount of discussion about the doors to the house, and which ones provided the easiest means of access, as well as what signs should be left behind to indicate that Voice

Number One had paid his visit. Voice Number One was concerned whether the side door would be locked.

> **V2:** It won't be locked. One of them may be
> hung up. You may go, oh fuck, fuck it,
> you may get hung up. If it does stick, it
> may get hung up.

After more discussion, Voice Number One asked Voice Number Two what he does when he comes home and the side door sticks.

> **V1:** Like, when you come home, and it gets
> hung up, what do you do?
> **V2:** I don't even bother with it, I go around to
> the other side.

Voice Number One mumbled something, but Voice Number Two responded:

> **V2:** Okay? Maybe if I jiggle it for fifteen
> minutes, it'll come loose, but why should I
> when I go around the other side?
> **V1:** Okay.
> **V2:** You know what I'm saying?
> **V1:** Okay.
> **V2:** Okay. Now what you need to do is rewrite
> this.
> **V1:** Uh-huh.
> **V2:** With corrections. Right now.
> **V1:** Uh-huh.

Now came the sound of paper going into a type-writer.

V2: And we're going to keep doing it until
you've got it right.
V1: No, we'll do it right now. I'll read out
what I'm doing.
V2: Oh, I gotta see—
V1: What? You gotta see what? You gotta
leave or something?
V2: No, I don't have to do anything.
V1: I gotta see your alarm.
V2: I've got that.

After more discussion about the alarm system, Voice Number Two apparently drew a diagram of the alarm system.

The sounds of a typewriter could be heard, including a repeated keypress like the drawing of a line. The typing lasted about three minutes, and ended with the sound of a piece of paper being removed from the typewriter.

V1: Okay?

After some additional low murmurs, Voice Number Two speaks:

V2: Look, Roger.
V1: Yeah.

The two voices had yet another discussion about

the alarm system, and referred to an earlier incident in which Voice Number One has accidentally tripped the alarm attempting to enter the house. Voice Number One explained what he thought happened in the earlier incident, but Voice Number Two says he's got it wrong.

> **V2:** No, what happened was, you hit 0003—
> I've done it, I've checked it out . . . okay,
> then it started yelling and making noise,
> and then it had cleared it up. It cleared . . .
> Right over this button. Same place as on
> your phone.
> **V1:** Yeah.
> **V2:** Okay.
> **V1:** So I press clear?
> **V2:** Clear. And then say, disarm, with the code.
> It's all very logical.

Voice Number One mumbled something.

> **V2:** Fifty seconds, to put in 00032. Boom, it's
> off.
> **V1:** Okay.

As the tape continued, Voice Number Two continued to instruct in the operation of the alarm.

> **V1:** Okay. Enter code?
> **V2:** This is what shows up: To arm, enter code.

Telling you, that when you leave, guess
what, "to arm, enter code."

After more discussion, it became apparent that
there were two possibilities that Voice Number One
would have to cope with once he reached the point
of entry, the side door—the alarm might have been
turned on by the occupant as the occupant was leaving; or alternatively, the alarm might have been left
off. What Voice Number One must *not* do is change
the situation in any way, in order to keep from warning the occupant when "she" returns that something
had changed.

Whether to disarm and rearm depended on whether
the alarm had actually been set when Voice Number
One first made his entry.

V2: I'm not telling you to do anything. I'm just
telling you what it will be. Or do anything.

Voice Number One mumbled again.

V2: Uhm, all you have to do is hit "leave,"
then it says, "to arm, enter code."
V1: 00032.
V2: Then it will go beep. Now you'll hear it
arm, and it will read in print, "Fifty seconds to exit" . . . beep . . . beep . . . beep . . .
V1: Okay. Okay.
V2: "Fifty seconds to exit" . . . beep . . . like
that. And then after fifty seconds . . .

Voice Number One asked a question, apparently about the motion detectors in the house.

V2: They shut off by the back room. Let's go over that. The back room door's gotta be closed.

V2: Yeah, but if you restore and arm that thing, she will close it. And there's also a fuck up there that could happen. She could forget to do that.

V1: That's what I'm saying, I gotta forget the hit?

V2: No!

The discussion now centered around whether it was a good idea for Voice Number One to rearm the alarm once he'd entered the house. Voice Number One now thought not.

V1: So rearming is just not a good idea.

V2: No.

V1: The bottom line is, it's just not a good idea. She sounds like she's not . . .

V2: No, but she's not gonna . . . Look, after what happened last week, it's an automatic reaction, though, when she arms it, and leaves, and says good night, and she walks back in, and it's not on, I mean . . .

V1: She's a lot more aware, then.

V2: Oh, much more aware, if the alarm's not on.

V1: Okay. Let's face it then. We gotta be on.
It's on . . .

V2: Okay. That's the simplest reason why it
should be on. We don't have any way to
fuck it up.

Voice Number One still didn't get it. If it was
armed and he turned it off, should he leave it off?

V2: No, no, no. You've gotta make sure you
haven't done anything different to the
house after you've armed it. When she
walks in, she arms it, with the back door
closed.

More mumbling came from Voice Number One.

V2: Right. But, she could fuck up. We're talking about all the possibilities here. You left
the door open and the dog ran out and for
some reason the dog wasn't moving enough
to set it off. Maybe she was asleep.

V1: Whatever, okay.

V2: Okay. So when you come in the back, you
need to look and make sure that [the alarm
is on].

V1: Okay.

V2: You disarm.

V1: Yeah, I understand. Now let me go back. I
want to rearm. "Leave." Okay?

V2: "To arm, enter code."

V1: "To arm, enter code." Triple 032. Okay?

Then the red light will come on with the
green light, and—

There was more mumbling between the voices.

V2: That's all I'm saying. You carry on.
V1: Then there's nothing more for me to do.
V2: Unless you change your mind.
V1: No, no, no. I'm gonna be honest. Make
sure those double doors are bolted, and I
go in the washroom first.
V2: Yeah.

The two voices discussed the possible movements
of the target inside the house.

V2: You know what I think I'd do? I think I'd
hear her coming in. Now let's remember,
there's sliding kitchen doors. It's open. She
comes in from the side of the driveway,
there's a light . . .

More discussion ensued about the previous attempt
to get inside the house.

V1: I went by afterwards, you know, and there
was another house about four or five doors
down. And it looked like your house . . .
Who knows? Maybe I screwed up. Because
you said there was no one parked in front
of your place? And I'm going like—
V2: All there was was a bunch of Mexicans
cutting grass two doors down. You remem-

ber seeing anybody cutting grass?

V1: No, I don't remember that.

Now the discussion turned to how to shoot someone.

V2: As long as she walks in the door, you got her.

V1: This is like a shotgun, you know what I'm saying?

Voice Number Two seemed worried that the target might escape.

V1: Uhm, I don't think so, because it'll be one-two-three. Just like that . . . boom, right there.

V2: What do you mean one-two-three?

V1: She's down.

V2: You mean you're telling me that by the third one you shoot her that—

V1: She's down on the floor now, in my opinion. Look, boom boom boom. And then, when she's down, when she's out, I go up to her, I finish it. And believe me, she can't live through that.

V2: Yeah, I understand that.

Voice Number Two wondered whether the target might be able to outmaneuver the shooter.

V1: Oh, of course, but see, once she's down, I can walk normal . . . I go like this, press, and fire . . . I use the light and it's incredible. I mean, it's accurate a hundred percent. Where that light goes, the bullet goes. It's gonna go.

The voices now discussed other options.

V1: What about hitting her at the top of the stairs?
V2: Yeah, what about it?
V1: At the top of the stairs, I got her; if she's in the vestibule area, I got her; and—
V2: You don't want her falling back against the front doors.
V1: Uh—
V2: They'd shatter.
V1: They would?

Now the voices talked about what to do if Voice Number One is discovered in the house before he can fire.

V2: You haven't done anything yet, either, have you?
V1: No, but I'm there and I'm armed. [Laughs]
V2: You haven't done anything. Have you?
V1: No.
V2: What happens if that happens, you walk back out. Get in your car and start the engine and . . .
V1: [Won't she know there's] something wrong?
V2: You haven't done anything, you haven't

wrecked the inside or anything else. You're
. . . out the back door.

V1: I'm out the back door, where do I go?

V2: I don't need to know that.

V1: Where do I go?

V2: Go back and sit in your own place.

V1: Or whatever the heck. Yeah. "Go back and
sit in your own place." I gotta go. I gotta
fucking go. Which blows the whole thing
with the house forever.

V2: Assuming you don't blow her away, that
you just don't go out the front door and
just blow her.

V1: How close should I get?

V2: That's up to you! You realize there's no
chance of faking, no chance of running—

V1: Out in front of the house, what am I gonna
do?

V2: No . . . hey, you don't need to stay, you
don't need—

V1: Look, I'd rather not rummage, if you want
to know the truth.

V2: Then don't.

V1: It's gonna cost me time.

V2: Good.

The voices return to the ring again, and whether
there ought to be some show of burglary, even a little
bit.

V1: I can't pull just one drawer out, I gotta go
through the place a little bit. I know there's

nothing in that drawer, you showed me.

V2: You can [wait] in the library, but you'd better not fucking move.

V1: Why the library?

V2: You're talking about the library in the back?

V1: Yeah.

V2: No, no, I'm talking about the library in the front.

V1: Right.

V2: Front room, right by the front door.

V1: Okay.

V2: Okay.

V1: Oh, I see.

V2: That motion detector points from the corner, as you face the front of my house, the motion detector . . . boop boop boop points across the staircase. The motion detector, Roger, in the back library, comes all the way through the [hall], into the front library. By closing the back library doors, you have [complete movement?] in the front library. The other motion detector covers the foyer, the staircase, and the living room. This one [points] like this, and this one, way back there, [points] like that. This one comes through this one, and . . . okay? This one comes through the front door, the foyer, the living room, the foyer, and the staircase. So if they're both on, there's no way you can go anywhere in my

fucking house. You have to cross one or
the other. This one—

V1: That's a benefit.

V2: But this one does not get the front library
either . . .

V1: I'll tell you what the downside is. The
downside of arming it—say . . . What's the
downside? Comes in—

V2: The downside of it is, [voices run together]
you have to back away from her to close
the door.

V1: Right.

V2: Now the possibility is that she won't close
the door after she activates it.

V1: Disarms it herself?

V2: Sure.

V1: Oh.

V2: What happens if she fucks up with it?

V1: Well—

V2: Two things could happen. She . . . so by the
time she gets her fuckin' hands on it in the
right way, immediately, you're cool. Now
you come out of the shadows and you hear
one, two, three, four, five. . . . You come
out, and the thing goes, beep! She hit the
wrong button! And she [unintelligible] you
hear what I'm saying?

V1: Whatever, yeah.

V2: You got me? And now you're dead. So—
you have actually got to wait—

V1: No, I'm not dead. I gotta go, I gotta hit her
right then and there without it—

V2: Right. Right.

V1: Anyway there's no—

V2: That's true. Or—

V1: Or what?

V2: Or—when she disarms, you got to wait to
hear her, you're waiting, you're waiting for
the green light to come on, and then you
start walking. You actually have to stop
and wait until you hear her move away.
Before you do anything. It's critical. By the
time she starts moving away, listen, just for
a second here, you can always [do it] on
the staircase.

V1: I understand. You want it on the staircase?

V2: No. No. But [you're] gonna have to shoot
her in the back.

Voice Number One says not necessarily, he could
always yell and have her turn around.

V2: On the way up the staircase?

The voices now discuss what the police will con-
clude from the angle of the firing if the target is shot
on the staircase, especially if she's shot in the back.
After a few more words, the tape runs out.

TWENTY-TWO

So what did all this interminable, static-ridden, obscure discussion of alarms and doors, motion detectors, places to wait, and alternative scenarios really mean?

From the point of view of Ferguson and Novak, the tape was damning in the extreme. The voices on the tape had all the pointers: the actual alarm code, a description of the house ("side door," the kitchen, placement of the motion detectors, "the office"), along with Voice Number Two's reference to "my house," "when I come home," "Roger," "she" in reference to the target, and even, at one point, "Doris" by name, at least according to the police version, although that could have been a confusion with the word "doors."

In any event, Ferguson and Novak had no doubt that the taped conversation was between Roger and Bob, if not from the sound of the voices, then from the content of the conversation.

But why? Why would Roger (presumably, since it was he who had possession of the tape in his briefcase) covertly tape his own brother—especially since the tape apparently implicated both brothers in a murder plot?

As Ferguson and Novak later came to believe, along with prosecutors Ted Wilson and Lyn McClellan, the tape was meant to be an insurance policy to make sure Bob paid off on the contract with Roger.

Doris was dead, and Roger, after his experience with
Bob and the book from 1990–1991, wanted to make
sure that he had something to hold Bob's feet to the
flames if he ever balked on paying what he owed. It
was only Roger's "screwup," as Ferguson later put
it, when Roger was arrested in Las Vegas, that caused
the insurance tape to come to light.

"There's no doubt in my mind, whatsoever, that
it's Bob on the tape," Ferguson said later. "Bob talks
about things that only the owner of the house would
know. He gives the alarm code out, 00032. He gives
the gate code out, 8134. These are numbers that we
felt only the homeowner would know. He talks about
what Doris normally does when she comes home. She
comes in the front door, and goes to the bathroom,
and then she goes to the back of the house. He wants
her dead. It's very, very cold. Like I said before,
there's no doubt whatsoever that it's Bob on that tape
discussing his wife."

But doubt was to be raised, and in a way that Ferguson could never, that July 28, ever have believed
possible.

With the tape, with the "my contract with you is the
kill and no squeeling" document, with Bob's behavior seeming to match the suggestions made by Roger
in his briefcase notes, and with a very big motive—
a divorce that promised to destroy Bob's very lucra-
tive betting business—the detectives believed they
had solved the murder of Doris Angleton.

It was, they told prosecutor Ted Wilson, a case of
contract murder, with Roger doing the killing in re-

turn for money from his brother, Bob. If you believed that the contents of Roger's briefcase reflected the true state of affairs between the brothers, rather than the supposed extortion being claimed by Bob, all the pieces fit.

But while it all might seem very logical, the facts themselves were very thin. The only inculpatory link between Roger and Bob was the tape, and since nowhere on the tape was Bob's name used, it could well be argued that it wasn't Bob at all, but someone else who just happened to sound like him.

Something more definite connecting the brothers in a conspiracy to commit murder was needed. So far, Ferguson and Novak hadn't been able to come up with anything—no records of telephone calls, no letters (they were still unaware of Jennifer Manning's activities), no evidence that Bob had provided anything to Roger other than the back of his hand.

"We tried and we tried and we tried," Ferguson said later. "We could not find that connection. We know they were making contact with each other, over mobile pagers, and by phone and stuff like that." But Ferguson and Novak could find no way to prove this.

Ferguson and Novak were convinced in their own minds that Roger had gotten the $64,282 in his possession in Las Vegas from Bob, but there were no records to prove that, either. After all, Bob dealt in large amounts of cash, most of it in safe-deposit boxes. It would have been simple to peel off a wad or two and pass it to Roger before or right after the murder.

The cash itself had been placed into custody by

the Las Vegas police, who promptly deposited the bills in an account when they believed it was drug money. So the bills themselves were no longer available for fingerprinting.

There was, however, an envelope in Roger's briefcase that contained several money wrappers. It was possible that the wrappers had once been around the money, and that they might hold some fingerprints. The wrappers were taken to the police lab for examination.

The following day, the results came in: One of the wrappers contained Bob's fingerprints.

Just before noon on the following day, Bob was driving to the drugstore not far from his house. He did not notice that he was being followed.

When he emerged a few minutes before 11:00 A.M., Ferguson and Novak approached him.

"Mr. Angleton," Ferguson said, "we have a warrant for your arrest on the charge of capital murder." It was Ali and Niki's thirteenth birthday, but Bob was going to jail.

TWENTY-THREE

Bob's arrest created a sensation in Houston.

"BROTHERS NABBED IN RIVER OAKS KILLING," the *Chronicle* trumpeted, "nabbed" being a word that apparently resonated in south Texas, instead of the more pedestrian "arrested."

In the scramble to get the story, however, some

facts were mixed up. A police spokesperson said that Roger had been brought back from Las Vegas, but that wasn't so; he was still in jail in the desert city. The paper said the police said that Roger had been stopped "at an airport in another state for trying to carry a weapon past an airport checkpoint," which was a triple garble, since Roger could hardly have been in another state on the same night he allegedly murdered Doris; obviously, Roger's Dallas-Fort Worth airport checkpoint "screwup" had somehow been conjoined with the murder date and Roger's June 22 arrest in Las Vegas.

The most interesting aspect of the "BROTHERS NABBED" story, however, was that the police were reported to believe that "her husband sent her home to get the bat," a reference to the softball bat left out on the deck at the rear of the house. This was the first public indication of the police theory tying Bob to the conspiracy: that he'd placed the bat on the deck in order to lure Doris to her death at the hands of Roger.

More came forth the following day. In "ANATOMY OF A GRISLY HOMICIDE, *Chronicle* reporter Eric Hanson tracked down the arrest warrant for Bob, and was rewarded with the first public mention of what would soon be called the "Brothers Tape."

Hanson said the tape contained the voices of two men discussing the planning of Doris' murder, and the alarm codes at the River Oaks house. Detectives Ferguson and Novak had sworn they believed that the voices on the tape were those of Roger and Bob, Hanson said.

Lieutenant Zoch of the homicide unit told Hanson

the detectives didn't know who made the recording, or why. That wasn't exactly true, since by this point, Ferguson and Novak were pretty clear that Roger had made the tape, in case Bob stiffed him.

Zoch said the police were at a loss to explain why Bob had given his own brother as a suspect if in fact the two were in on the conspiracy from the beginning.

"That has bugged us constantly," Zoch said.

In the meantime, a prominent Houston lawyer, Mike Ramsey, had been retained to defend Bob. At 57, Ramsey was regarded as one of the most potent defenders in the state; he had begun his career by studying with legendary Texas lawyers Percy Foreman and Richard "Racehorse" Haynes.

In addition to being perhaps the best criminal defense lawyer money could buy in Houston, Ramsey's selection was a natural, since he shared his office space with George Tyson, Bob's longtime lawyer.

By Monday, three days after Bob's arrest, Ramsey was already swinging into action.

"I don't think the guy did it," he told a reporter for the *Chronicle*. "I think he has a crazy brother."

Just how crazy was Roger?

"He's crazy as a lunatic," Ramsey said, noting that Roger had been known to dress up like a rabbit and go out in public.

Well, it was true that Roger had once dressed as a rabbit, but it was for a Halloween party. Ramsey made it sound like Roger was some sort of homicidal version of Harvey, the imaginary rabbit made famous by Jimmy Stewart.

Four days later, Ramsey tried to get Bob out on bail, an effort opposed by Harris County prosecutors Wilson and McClellan.

"He's got a lot of money," Wilson said. "If I were out on bond and if I were looking on a finding of guilt at either the death penalty or forty years' flat time, I wouldn't hang around."

To support their demand that Bob be kept in jail, the prosecutors played the Brothers Tape, and had Ferguson read from the notes found in Roger's briefcase. Ferguson and Novak both testified that the voices on the tape were those of Roger and Bob.

Ramsey was ready for this; in addition to demanding that the tape be examined by experts to determine whether it had been altered, Ramsey called a half-dozen of Bob's acquaintances, including Tex Welsh, to testify that they could not swear that the voice on the tape was Bob's.

At the conclusion of the hearing, however, Judge Brian Rains denied Bob bail. Ramsey said the defense would appeal.

One week later, San Diego Police Department officers, acting on a warrant obtained by the San Diego County District Attorney's Office, arrived at Jennifer Manning's house in San Diego.

As Ferguson later put it, having reached the conclusion that Roger recorded the Brothers Tape as a form of insurance against possible double-dealing by Bob, it was only logical to suspect that other tapes might exist as well. And if Jennifer was Roger's "designee," wasn't it likely that if there were more tapes or other evidence, it might be found near Jennifer?

"We just felt that Roger had told her her quite a bit about this killing, and was even holding evidence, like more tapes, or even the murder weapon," Ferguson said.

McClellan took this reasoning even further, noting that if Roger had made an earlier attempt to kill Doris—as the tape and the notes seemed to suggest—it was likely that there was also an earlier Brothers tape. What if Roger had succeeded in killing Doris on April 10? Wouldn't he have his insurance ready before he acted, as he seemed to have done for the successful attempt on April 16?

Even more to the point was a notation on one of the scraps of paper taken from Roger's briefcase, abjuring someone to "protect the tapes." The use of the word "tapes" seemed to indicate that there was more than one.

In their affidavit in support of the search, the San Diego authorities noted that Jennifer had been less than forthcoming with Ferguson, at least in Ferguson's opinion.

"Jennifer Ann Manning was not cooperative with Ferguson and did not provide any meaningful information about Roger Angleton and, in the opinion of your affiant, was assisting Roger Angleton, prior to his arrest, to elude capture. Further, it is the opinion of Ferguson that Roger Angleton has been in continuous contact with Jennifer Ann Manning both while eluding capture and while continuing to be in contact with her as of the making of this affidavit . . .

"It is the opinion of Ferguson . . . based on the notes found in the briefcase concerning the payout for the murder, the passports, and the note that Jennifer Manning delivered to Robert Angleton's business, that the tapes referred to in the note are being held by Jennifer Manning and are located within the home that she and Roger Angleton share in San Diego . . ."

The search produced two microcasette recorders, each with a tape inside, and two more microcasettes from a drawer in the master bedroom. None of the four shed any light on Doris' murder, however; and there were no weapons found in the house, let alone the murder gun.

TWENTY-FOUR

While authorities were looking for but failing to find any other Brothers tapes, the brothers themselves remained in jail. Roger was still in Las Vegas, pending extradition on the Texas murder warrant, and Bob was awaiting the outcome of his lawyer Ramsey's appeal of the judge's order denying him bail.

Against this backdrop, the Houston police now conducted a new search of Bob's house on Ella Lee Lane.

This search was later to become a critical turning point in the case against Robert Angleton; simply put, in hindsight, the police and the prosecutors may have made a major blunder by limiting what they sought in their search.

For some time, Assistant District Attorney Wilson had been wondering whether the police might find Roger's fingerprints on the safe in Bob's bedroom; or, whether they might find Roger's prints in Bob's private bookmaking office, which was around to the rear of the house, accessible only by its own entrance. Wilson believed it was possible that Roger had waited in the office for Doris and the girls to leave, then entered the house while they were gone. In addition, there was a need to inspect the alarm system and the motion detectors to see whether they corresponded with the description of the system found on the Brothers Tape. So Wilson drafted a search warrant for the Ella Lee house.

Unfortunately, Wilson's warrant was limited to a search for the fingerprints and the alarm system; given that Ferguson and Novak had been laboring for months to prove that some sort of sub-rosa connection between Roger and Bob existed, it's rather surprising that a third item was not added to the search list—any papers, letters, tape recordings, telephone messages or other such documentary evidence tending to show that Roger and Bob had been in communication after the murder. The oversight was to cost the prosecutors later.

Ferguson and Novak executed the warrant. They went upstairs to the bedroom where the safe was. It was while the safe was being dusted for prints that one or the other of the detectives noticed a drawer that Ferguson later contended was partially open. Inside the drawer, the detectives found the two messages to Bob from Roger, the ones that had been delivered via Jennifer Manning and Tex Welsh, the messages that had prompted Bob to reply by way of the post office box in Monarch Beach, the messages that neither Jennifer nor Bob had ever told the police about.

The longer of the notes was the one Jennifer Manning had typed at Roger's instructions back in July, and included Roger's representation to Bob that he was committed to their arrangement up to and including suicide, provided that Bob fulfill his end of the deal.

This longer note from Roger, in Ferguson's view, thus contained statements that tended to show that Bob, far from being a victim of his "crazy" brother, was actually a full participant in the conspiracy. Ferguson believed that Bob hadn't shown the detectives either of the notes because he didn't want to have to answer any questions about them.

"There was some information in the long letter that he didn't want us to see," Ferguson said afterward. "All this is a little too much between Bob and Roger," for Bob's comfort, Ferguson thought.

Delighted with this discovery, which they believed linked Bob definitely to the plot, the detectives seized both messages, only to learn later that they had exceeded their authority.

"Basically, what happened was this," Wilson said later. "The search warrant allowed them to go up and fingerprint the safe, over here. It doesn't give them the right to start over and go looking over there.

"Here's the thing," he added. "We had never known that thing [the documents] was there. I don't fault them [Novak and Ferguson] for opening up a drawer, they're inquisitive, that's why they're there, to do what they do. And that's why I like their inquisitive minds. But the fact is, we can't get there from here, legally. And so, here we have this thing, and we couldn't put it in."

That meant the two messages from Roger to Bob—the only documented communications between the brothers after the murder—would have to be excluded from evidence, because they were beyond the scope of the search warrant.

Later, the police blamed the court for the exclusion of the evidence; but the fact is, the warrant was poorly drafted to begin with. The situation was one factor that led to some strained relations between the District Attorney's office and the police as the case proceeded; there would be other strains, as well, as time went on.

Although Ramsey had been expecting a quick ruling from the Texas Court of Appeals on Bob's request for bail—he told the *Chronicle* that the search of the Ella Lee house might be an attempt to get more evidence on Bob and thus influence the appeals court—the ruling did not come down until the end of October.

In a 2-1 decision, the court held that Bob *was* entitled to bail.

Under Texas state law, Bob would ordinarily have been entitled to bail unless his guilt was "evident," a legal standard just below the highest standard, "beyond a reasonable doubt."

Two of the justices who heard Bob's appeal agreed with Mike Ramsey that the law required the prosecutors to show who made the Brothers Tape, how, and when. Without such a foundation, the tape should have been ruled inadmissable at Bob's August bail hearing. Without the tape, the justices said, proof of Bob's guilt was no longer "evident," and thus, bail should be granted.

But this victory for Bob was short-lived. Immediately after the ruling, the District Attorney's office filed an appeal to the Court of Criminal Appeals in Austin. Bob would remain in jail until that appeal was resolved.

In the meantime, the detectives had been working to pin down the locations of Bob's stashes of cash; since Bob had admitted he was a bookmaker to the police, the reasoning was that the cash might be seized by the police as the proceeds of illegal activity.

On the day of the search of the Ella Lee house, district attorney's investigator Margaret Jewell received a report from a bank security officer, who contended that he had seen Bob in the Frost Bank on April 24, eight days after the murder.

According to the guard, Bob came into the bank and asked an official there about renting a safe-deposit box. The security guard said that Bob spoke loudly and asked a number of questions about records the bank kept on box customers, whether he had to sign to get access to his box, and whether anyone besides him would have a key. After renting two boxes, Bob refused to provide his home address or any telephone number where he might be reached.

Several hours later, according to the security guard, Bob returned to the bank with a briefcase and a leather satchel that appeared to be heavy. Bob went into the safe-deposit area, and emerged some minutes later with the now considerably lighter satchel and briefcase.

"Well," the security guard remembered Bob saying, "you won't be seeing me again for another five years."

This information seemed to indicate that Bob had a stash of cash in the Frost Bank. Jewell went to the bank to check out the story, and pulled the records on Boxes 107 and 207, as well as the bank's video tape for April 24, 1997. It was definitely Bob, and the records showed that no one had been in the bank to open the box since April 24.

On October 7, Ferguson went to the bank with a search warrant and had bank officials open Boxes 107 and 207, the first of which yielded the rather astonishing sum of $965,100, and the second another $965,300, for a grand total of $1,930,400, all in cash.

Now, some thought, even if Bob was granted bail and tried to flee, he'd be so short of money he might not be able to get very far. But the assumption that the police had found most of Bob's money was also wrong, as it turned out.

TWENTY-FIVE

By the end of October, a grand jury had indicted both Roger and Bob for Doris' murder. The jury heard the tape, and took testimony from Ferguson and Novak, as well as Ali and Niki, among others. The jurors also heard portions of a lengthy deposition from Jennnifer Manning. This set the stage for the completion of Roger's extradition from Las Vegas, and he arrived at the Harris County jail on November 19.

Meanwhile, Bob's lawyer Tyson was making a daily trek down to Wilson's office to read the official police file on the case. In Texas, these files could not be copied or removed from the District Attorney's premises; in some jurisdictions, in fact, defense lawyers weren't even allowed to see them.

"I started going down there in November," Tyson recalled. "It was a huge report, maybe two inches thick. Single spaced, typed. I'd read for two or three hours, take careful notes, then come back the next day and start all over again. It must have taken me eighty hours to read the whole thing over three months."

By examining the specifics of the police case against Bob and Roger, Tyson hoped to find holes in the evidence that could be widened into reasonable doubt.

For the first time Tyson discovered that the police ballistics laboratory had discovered that two different .22-caliber guns had been used in the murder. Indeed, there was some faintly suggestive evidence that possibly two shooters had been present in the house, judging from the fact that shell casings had been found on both sides of Doris' body, and the fact that at least one wound was in the front, while the rest were from the side or back.

Finally, Tyson noticed that the police had assembled a considerable amount of information on Roger's perambulations before and after the murder, including the fact that he had checked into several Houston hotels using a variety of aliases; witnesses at some of these places had told the police they had seen Roger in the company of a younger blond man.

Thus was born the "two-shooter" theory, as it came to be called; the defense would contend, and still contends, that there was a second gunman in the house on the night Doris was killed, and that the police rushed to judgment in concluding that Roger had done the deed all by himself.

The police, however, considered the suggestion laughable. As Wilson was later to point out, the hallway where Doris was killed was so narrow that if there had been two shooters, one on either side of Doris, the chances were excellent the two shooters would have shot each other as well as Doris.

Now began a strange twist to the Angleton murder case. Roger began to talk; and once he began talking, he didn't seem to be able to stop.

The repository for all this gabbing was Vanessa Leggett, a part-time writer from Austin who was on friendly terms with Roger's Houston lawyer, Mark Bennett. Over the next two months, Vanessa was to record over eighteen tapes, many three hours in length, of conversations with Roger in preparation for a book Vanessa wanted to write.

Vanessa actually first met Roger when he was in jail in Las Vegas. She flew to that city to interview him in October.

"He agreed to be interviewed," she said later, "and we established a rapport."

According to those who later heard Vanessa's Roger tapes—they eventually came to be caught up in the grinder of the criminal case—Roger's reminiscences rambled over a wide range of topics.

At one point, Roger told Vanessa that he had committed the murder, and at Bob's instigation; at another point, he claimed that he had done it on his own; at a third point, he said he hadn't committed the murder and didn't know who did, and at still another point suggested that the Mafia had killed Doris.

Much of the content of the tapes was concerned with the various cloak-and-dagger schemes so beloved by Roger; it seems that in Vanessa's tape recorder he'd finally found a place where he could command all the attention he craved.

Later, Steve Brewer, a reporter for the *Chronicle* who was familiar with the Roger tapes, joked that, given all his gabbing, it wouldn't have been surprising to find out that Roger was claiming he'd been on the grassy knoll in Dallas.

Still, according to those who heard the tapes, Roger did provide some corrobating evidence, including a description of what Roger said he did at the Ella Lee house that fairly well matched what the police had discovered or theorized.

Then, at the end of January, new attention was focused on Bob's bookmaking operation when the *Chronicle* reported that despite Bob's arrest, Bob's book was still operating, unabated.

In "GAMBLING RING STILL IN BUSINESS," the *Chronicle*'s S. K. Bardwell reported that bets were being taken by the same people who had worked for Bob before his arrest, and that even some of the same telephone numbers were in use.

Asked to explain, Houston Police Chief C. O. Bradford told Bardwell that he wasn't at all surprised to learn that Bob's book hadn't been busted because they had yet to make a case against him.

That was because the police had made the solution of Doris' murder a higher priority, Bradford indicated. And, once Bob had been arrested, an internal affairs investigation was conducted of Kevin Templeton, Bob's contact in the vice unit.

The investigation of Templeton was still continuing, even though an apparent earlier attempt to bring a "sting" operation against Templeton had been called off, Bardwell reported.

"I can tell you," Bradford told Bardwell, "I'm not satisfied that it has taken [internal affairs] this long to complete this.

"If [Angleton's] operation is continuing to go on, we need to make a case on the operation, working with the District Attorney's office, the vice cops, any kind of cops. I'd like to see the cops go out and make a case on Angleton and quit talking about it."

*   *   *

Making a case on Angleton was just what was on Assistant District Attorney Lyn McClellan's mind as January came to a close. McClellan had reviewed the evidence in the brothers' murder case and decided more was needed. He came up with a fiendishly ingenious plan to make sure that Bob was convicted: He would get Roger to testify against his own brother.

As McClellan later put it, he made an offer to Roger's lawyer, Mark Bennett.

"I met with Roger's lawyer to put an offer on the table," McClellan said, "and it went like this: Let's say we give your guy immunity [in return for his testimony against Bob]. And when our office sees what he testifies [to] in Robert's trial, that's it."

Immunity for anything Roger admitted to during the course of Bob's trial—such as an admission that he'd shot Doris at Bob's instigation—meant that the District Attorney's office could not use any of that testimony against Roger in his own trial.

And since the only real evidence against Roger was the materials found in the briefcase in Las Vegas—and that evidence was likely to be suppressed because of the bad search by the Las Vegas police, at least in McClellan's view—that meant, in effect, that Roger was likely to walk away from the murder charge entirely; in other words, the chances were quite good that Roger would wind up a free man if he testified against Bob.

Roger's lawyer, Mark Bennett, thought the idea was interesting. He conveyed it to Roger before leaving to go to New Jersey to try another case in that state. McClellan recalled that he and Bennett agreed to meet with Roger at the jail on February 6, 1998; Bennett's recollection was that no specific date had been set for the meeting.

When February 6 approached, McClellan said, Bennett called him from New Jersey to say he would not be back in Houston until the following week.

"I said, well, let's just roll it over 'til Monday," McClellan said, and in this version, Bennett agreed.

So it was with the very real prospect of walking away from the murder he had committed that Roger went to bed that Friday night in the Harris County jail.

But when jailers came to check up on Roger just after six on the following morning, Roger was dead. He'd bled to death from scores of cuts inflicted by tiny disposable razor blades across his neck, wrists, and lower legs. It was one year to the day that Doris Angleton had filed for divorce.

TWENTY-SIX

The floor of Roger's solitary cell was flooded with Roger's blood, which was also smeared on the wall. His jail uniform was soaked through. Before killing himself, Roger had placed two towels under the door to the cells to keep blood from leaking into the hallway outside. Around his body lay seven razor blades. Against the wall was a yellow legal pad filled with Roger's scrawling handwriting:

TO WHOM IT MAY CONCERN!!
IN THE EVENT OF MY DEATH PLEASE CALL

VANESSA LEGETT—SHE IS COMPLETELY EM-POWERED TO MAKE "FINAL ARRANGE-MENTS" REGARDING FINAL DISPOSITION OF MY BODY. HERE TELEPHONE #S ARE . . . (AL-WAYS AVAILABLE AT THOSE NUMBERS BE-TWEEN 7:00 AM TILL 10 PM)

I KILLED DORIS ANGLETON IN AN ULTIMATE ATTEMPT TO BEGIN AN EXTORTION PROGRAM BASED ON FEAR & THE THREAT OF FURTHER DEATH FROM [sic] ROBERT ANGLETON. ROB-ERT OWED ME MONEY BUT I REALIZE THAT I WAS WRONG TO TAKE A LIFE OF ESPECIALLY AN INNOCENT & GOOD PERSON. I AM IN CON-STANT EMOTIONAL AGONY AND SO DECIDED TO END MY LIFE TO STOP THE PAIN. AL-THOUGH, I BEGAN AN ELABORATE PLAN TO "FRAME" ROBERT FOR DORIS' DEATH AS FUR-THER LEVERAGE TO GET MY MONEY, HE IS IN-NOCENT.

ANYWAY, I DONATE MY BOOKS IN "PER-SONAL PROPERTY" AND IN MY CELL TO THE INMATES. I HOPE THIS TRAGEDY IN SOME WAY STOPS SOMEONE SOMEWHERE FROM COMMITTING PRE-MEDITATED MURDER, IT IS ONE OF THE FEW CRIMES IS IN FACT THE ONLY CRIME THAT CAN NEVER BE MADE RIGHT OR FORGIVEN. LIFE IS THE PROVI-DENCE OF GOD AND GOD ONLY AND I LEAVE THIS WORLD WITH THAT THOUGHT.

ROGER ANGLETON

SORRY FOR THE MESS

It turned out there were actually four such suicide notes, each addressed by Roger to different individuals, including Vanessa, Roger's lawyers, and a reporter for the *Chronicle*, George Flynn; apparently Roger meant for Flynn to turn this note over to Bob's lawyer Mike Ramsey. It appeared that Ramsey's name was added to the note some time after Roger had written it. The curious thing about this note was that it was dated February 1—six days before Roger actually killed himself:

> Houston Chronicle
> *To: George Flynn or Mike Ramsey*
> *Dear Mr. Flynn or Mr. Ramsey*
> *I shot Doris Angleton to death on April 16, 1997 in an attempt to create an extortion situation based on fear to gain money from my brother which I have felt he owed me. I also attempted to make it look as though he was part of it as further leverage & get big money. Now I know that I was wrong and can't live with myself and big pain any longer. The purpose of this letter is to let the truth be known.*
>
> > *Sincerely,*
> > *Roger Angleton*

Given the circumstances—Roger dying in the same jail that held his brother, and just after he'd been offered immunity to testify against Bob—it wasn't surprising that speculation soon arose that Roger's death was more than a simple case of suicide. Still, Bennett, Roger's lawyer, tried to envision how someone might have been able to kill Roger, and quickly concluded that it wasn't very likely.

For one thing, since Roger had been in administrative segregation—solitary confinement—that meant that a killer had to be a guard. It wasn't very likely that a guard could have killed Roger with seven tiny razor blades, inflicting over fifty separate cuts, without someone else noticing what he was up to. And, of course, there were the notes, which were obviously in Roger's own writing, including one dated February 1.

Harris County Sheriff Tommy Thomas said Roger had given no indication that he was suicidal.

"He appeared to be okay," Thomas told the *Chronicle*. "He had made no [prior] suicide attempts. His behavior indicated that he was not a suicide risk and our jail staff tells us that he had been upbeat in the days preceding this incident."

The immediate effect of Roger's death was to throw the case against Bob into a state of confusion. Ramsey, for one, suggested that since Roger had claimed all the responsibility for Doris' murder, Bob now should be granted bail.

"Roger had a documentable history of mental sickness," Ramsey said, "so this is not really a surprise to me that a guy in his mental condition would do something like that."

Ramsey said Bob had heard of Roger's death, and the contents of the suicide notes, with mixed emotions.

"They were blood enemies, but they were still brothers," Ramsey told the *Chronicle*. "His comment was, 'He finally told the truth.'

"It seems the things Robert has told the police are turning out to be true. I think our Harris County District Attorney's office are fair-minded people, and I hope we can reach an agreement on the bond."

The notes, Ramsey contended, should be viewed by the legal system as a "dying declaration" by Roger, and should therefore be admissible in any trial of Bob.

But McClellan wasn't so sure about that. He kept thinking about the notes found in Roger's briefcase, and the promises that Roger had made to Bob that he was in their deal "up to and including suicide," as McClellan put it.

McClellan formed a theory as to what had happened: Having put pressure on Roger with the proffer of immunity, Roger found himself with no other exit.

"You know, Roger had no reason to commit suicide to avoid prosecution, because Roger probably would never have been prosecuted," McClellan said later.

"I believe the reason he committed suicide [was because] he couldn't stand up to the cross-examination that he would be subjected to if he was to testify, under the immunity, that he'd done it to frame Bob.

"You know how it would go: 'Well, if that's the case, then what did you ever do to point to Bob as being involved?' Nothing. You cannot find me one thing he ever did to point to Bob. Everything was pointing toward Roger. Now, are you going to tell me that he got himself arrested in Las Vegas for using a false driver's license, knowing that what he had in his briefcase, a tape, and knowing that they're going to violate his rights [by the search of the briefcase]? No. That was an accidental deal. It was an *accident*.

"But, if you're going to frame somebody, you make that tape, you send it to HPD in a manila envelope and say, 'Guess who this is, Bubba.' You turn it over, you put it on a doorstep, you do whatever you have to [to implicate Bob]. There is nobody on this earth who can identify one thing Roger that pointed to Bob as the killer—except the stuff he was found with, accidentally, in Las Vegas.''

McClellan came to believe that Roger had simply, if fatally, fulfilled his part of the bargain with Bob.

''I think Roger was committed to the idea he was going to die. And I don't believe that Roger would ever have done that, would never have committed suicide, unless he knew for a fact, was guaranteed and shown to him, somehow, legally, that there's money in place, in some trust fund, that's going to cut checks, on designated dates, to the designated person, and nobody can go back and fuck it up.''

So in McClellan's view, Roger's suicide became inevitable, particularly with the immunity deal on the horizon.

''My theory is that it was all part of the plan. I mean, when you look at the notes that come out of the briefcase, talking about, my contract with you is to kill, and to give you an alibi, and make me the suspect, up to and including death. You're to pay money to me or my designee. Why do you need a designee? Why don't you just pay to me?

''Because I think he knew he was going to have to die. The question arises is, Why would one kill somebody for money, knowing that they're going to die, [and] take the blame for it? And the answer is, to me, is that he knew he was terminally ill.''

* * *

McClellan's idea was an interesting theory; Roger's autopsy later showed that his coronary arteries were severely blocked; in addition, his bad back was causing him constant pain. McClellan came to believe that living just wasn't worth the pain to Roger, and that he'd decided to make one big score, even if he had to kill himself to do it.

In McClellan's view, the plan between Roger and Bob changed after the arrest of Roger in Las Vegas. Where first the plan had been for Bob to claim that Roger had murdered Doris as part of an extortion plot against Bob, the scenario shifted after the arrest to include the notion that Roger intended to frame Bob for being involved in the murder that Roger was then suspected of committing, thus providing a cover explanation for the existence of the ''contract with you to kill and no squeeling.''

This would be the dividing line, over the next few months, between the prosecutors and Bob's defenders: McClellan claiming that Roger's confession and suicide was simply his part of the bargain with Bob, and Bob claiming that the whole thing was the product of Roger's deranged and desperate mind, obsessed with framing his brother as a furtherance of his initial attempt to extort money.

Indeed, everything in the case, except for the tape, could be read either way: Either it was a plot by Bob and Roger, or it was Roger's attempt to frame Bob.

TWENTY-SEVEN

Ramsey's hope that Roger's confession would clear the way for Bob's release on bail was soon dashed; the Harris County District Attorney's office opposed a renewed motion that Bob be released.

"We're not agreeing to a bond," McClellan said. "That is pending before the Court of Criminal Appeals."

Meanwhile, the police department's internal investigation of Kevin Templeton continued to proceed, however slowly. By early March, Templeton was cleared of any impropriety regarding his handling of Bob as an informant. Templeton had been charged with accepting bribes from Angleton while giving protection to Bob.

"We have completed an investigation," said Police Chief Bradford, "and those allegations were in fact not sustained."

Bradford did not say the allegations were unfounded, only that they couldn't be proven.

By late April, Ferguson had found still more of Bob's money. On April 24, he seized $1,490,200 in cash from a box at Citizens National Bank in Bellaire. The box had been in the name of DNA Investments. That brought the total so far seized from Bob to nearly $3.4 million. The money was seized as proceeds of illegal bookmaking and money laundering.

Ramsey, meanwhile, was trying to find a way to

suppress all of the evidence that Bob had stashed money in any safe-deposit box, including this new seizure; he elected to contend that the affidavit backing the searches was insufficient because Margaret Jewell, the district attorney's investigator who swore the affidavit "intentionally or recklessly omitted from her affidavits the fact that defendant had been an active informant for the vice department of the Houston Police Department for more than 10 years concerning gambling operations in the city of Houston."

In other words, the police had known all along about Bob's bookmaking activity, and the fact of Bob's cooperation with the vice unit showed that Bob's bookmaking activity hardly constituted new information; indeed, the very fact that police had known for so long of Bob's book was a defense against charges that the money had been illegally obtained and laundered. The judge denied Ramsey's motion, and the cash remained in the state's coffers for the time being.

For some time, Ted Wilson had been worrying about the key evidence against Bob, the tape. Wilson knew that Ramsey was a resourceful lawyer, and that Bob was wealthy. It stood to reason that Bob's defenders would make every effort to somehow prove that it wasn't Bob on the tape.

"Here's what happened," Wilson said later. "I got to figuring, because of the amount of money that this defendant had, we had to gird ourselves up for a real dogfight."

Wilson was sure that Ramsey would find some

expert who would try to scientifically prove that it wasn't Bob's voice. Wilson was vaguely aware of a technology which could compare voice prints for identification purposes, even if legal precedents on the technology's use in court were split. He guessed that Ramsey would find such an expert for Bob.

"I didn't know anything about voice identification, and so I sat down on the Internet and started playing with it, to find out what the Internet had to tell me," Wilson said. "And I learned something about the mechanics of it, and then I started looking for who could do it."

Wilson soon came across Steve Cain, a former forensic expert for the IRS, the Secret Service, and the FBI. Cain had established his own laboratory in Wisconsin, and developed something of a specialty in voice identification.

"Steve Cain was very impressive from his résumé," Wilson said. "So I went down and talked to the district attorney and suggested that maybe we needed to do this, because I would bet you *they're* going to do something like this."

Harris County District Attorney Johnny Holmes agreed to Wilson's proposal to hire Cain.

"I said to him, can you do this? Can you enhance it for us? He and I discussed, you know, how do you compare it? Well, you do it by exemplar, and we talked at some length about that."

To be legally valid, Cain explained, a comparison would have to be made with an authenticated Bob's voice repeating the words and phrases on the tape taken from Roger's briefcase. It wouldn't be legally sufficient for Cain to simply compare the known Bob's voice on the 911 or the Wright tapes with the Roger tape, because the same words and phrases were not involved. That meant someone would have to isolate various phrases from the Roger tape, and make up a list for Bob to repeat for the purposes of comparison.

"Then we got a court order to take the exemplar," Wilson said. "Cain did not come down here to do it. Homicide detectives took it for him. And when you listen to the examplar, frankly, my feeling is, it doesn't sound like Bob at all."

To provide the exemplar, Bob was taken to the homicide offices, where Stan Schneider, one of his lawyers, was waiting. Ferguson said across the table from Bob, and told him to "repeat the phrase just as I say it," as Schneider recalled.

"There were twenty-six phrases, and Bob had to repeat each of them three times. He did exactly what Ferguson asked." Not only did Bob repeat after Ferguson seventy-eight times, he also read each phrase from the list seventy-eight times.

"Ferguson would listen to the questioned tape and repeat it, and Bob would repeat it back to him," Wilson said. "The problem was, Bob is from New Jersey and Ferguson's from Louisiana, and their voices aren't even close to being alike. So if I'm sitting there trying to mimic Ferguson, I'm not going to be even close [to what he would ordinarily sound like]."

Wilson later came to believe Bob deliberately tried to sabotage the exemplar by aping Ferguson's drawl. Ferguson thought so, too.

In any event the Roger tape and the exemplar were

sent to Cain, along with several microcassette recorders that had been found in Roger's or Jennifer's possession. Wilson hoped to be able to get around Ramsey's certain objection to the admissibility of the tape, since no one was now available to testify as to how, when, and where it was made, now that Roger was dead. Ideally, Wilson hoped that Cain would be able to testify that Voice Number Two had to be Bob.

Wilson sent Cain $3,000 for his expert services. Several weeks went by without Wilson hearing anything. Then Cain called Wilson.

"Cain calls me up, and he says, look, I've finished," Wilson said afterward. "And he says, I've got some bad news. And I say, what's that?

"And he says, he can't say that's Bob. And I say, Well, okay. What can you say? Well, I'm not seeing any similarity at all. I say, Well, okay. Are you telling me it's *not* Bob? He says, No, I'm not telling you it's not Bob. I say, Okay, I can live with that. So you're not saying it's not, you just can't say it is? He said, That's right. I say, okay, well, fine. I need a copy of your report, Steve, because I'm going to have to provide it to the defense. Understand that they'll probably try to contact you about this. It's up to you whether you want to talk to them or not."

Cain's report was dated the first of July 1998.

"An aural and spectrographic examination of the submitted tape evidence," Cain wrote, "disclosed a number of aural and spectrographic dissimilarities between the examined voices. Accordingly, the opinion rendered in this voice identification is: *possible elimination*—at least 80 percent of comparable words are

very dissimilar aurally and spectrographically pro-
ducing not less than ten words that do not match.''

So much for the bright idea of having an expert
authenticate Bob's voice, Wilson thought. At least no
one will be able to give expert testimony that it's
demonstrably not Bob's voice.

"So he sent me this report, and he was in a hurry,
because, he says, I'm getting married and I'm leaving
in about two days. So I get this report, and it's about
two lines. So I give it to the defense.''

Wilson had been right, because Bob's team of lawyers had been considering hiring a voice expert; they
also had been doing legal research on the prospect of
challenging the legal validity of voice identification
if the state tried to use it to prove that it was Bob's
voice on the tape.

Now Ramsey and Tyson were delighted to receive
a copy of Cain's report from McClellan.

The next thing Wilson knew, Cain was back on
the telephone with him.

"What surprised me then was that Cain calls me
back and says, the defense wanted to hire him,'' Wilson recalled. "Well, I say, I can't tell you no, but man,
I'm sitting there thinking, I don't mind you talking to
them if you want to, that's fine, I'm willing to be fair
about this, but it seems kind of odd that he's taking my
money and then he's going to turn around and take
more from them. Which is exactly what he did.''

Ramsey's team hired Cain to be their own expert.
Since the state had originally hired Cain, in effect,
Ramsey was now able to use the state's own expert
witness against them.

This was, to say the least, a bitter blow to the prosecution.

"When Cain's report came in," McClellan recalled, "I figured there's no chance in hell, because we're dealing with a real good lawyer, and Ramsey's thing is reasonable doubt, and if ever an expert raised reasonable doubt, Cain had."

TWENTY-EIGHT

As the date for the selection of the jury for Bob's trial neared, both sides began efforts to shape the evidence that would be presented for the jury's consideration.

Both sides began with a stipulation, an agreement, that all of the handwritten documents found in Roger's briefcase or his suitcase would be considered as emanating from Roger's own hand. The typewritten documents were a different story, however; Ramsey wanted all of them excluded because there was no way to show who had composed them.

That was as true of the documents found in the briefcase as it was the typed notes found in Bob's closet.

Margaret Jewell, the district attorney's investigator, went to Seattle to reinterview Jennifer Manning Angleton, and to serve her with a subpoena to testify at the trial. According to both McClellan and Ferguson, Jennifer—who had divorced Roger at the end of 1997, ending what turned out to be a six-month marriage, most of it with Roger in jail—at first continued to insist that she knew nothing of the communications between Roger and Bob.

"So Peg Jewell went out there," McClellan said. "Vanessa Leggett had talked to her—they were good friends—Vanessa Leggett had talked to her the day before, and so, she was congenial, said she doesn't owe Bob anything, doesn't have sides in this deal, doesn't have a dog in this hunt. Initially, [to Jewell] she said she didn't recall what the content [of the messages to Bob] was, then the next morning she said that she did."

Jennifer now told Jewell about Roger's holding the paper up in the jail, and her copying the words down to type and send to Bob via Roadrunner, and about the Monarch Beach post office boxes.

Jewell returned to Houston with this news, which now promised a possible way to get the notes found in Bob's closet in front of the jury, since Jennifer could testify as to their origin. Jewell went to Roadrunner and showed the notes to Tex Welsh. Did he recall ever having seen those before? Tex was asked.

Tex nodded. He'd faxed them to Bob in Lahaina. Jewell now knew how the notes had come to be in Bob's closet.

But why hadn't Tex come forward before? Jewell formed the impression that he was talking only because Jennifer had told the story. Jewell later reported back to Wilson and McClellan that Tex said of the notes, "I knew it was evil."

There it was again, that two-sided blade: what was evil, Roger's plan to frame Bob, or Bob's plot with Roger? It depended on how you looked at it.

*   *   *

Although the prosecution wanted to get as much of the evidence in as they could, they also wanted to stay as far away as possible from Roger's suicide. The situation was exactly the opposite for the defense.

Wilson and McClellan argued that the suicide notes were hearsay evidence, and that no exception existed for them to be brought before the jury; Ramsey argued that Roger's notes were admissible because they were statements made by Roger which implicated himself in Doris' death, and that they were "excited utterances" made under emotional conditions, and also that they were "dying declarations," the idea being that if a person was about to die, he or she would be most likely to tell the truth.

In a way the controversy mirrored the entire case: The prosecutors believed that the suicide and the notes showed that Roger was prepared to keep his bargain with Bob, "up to and including suicide," and by falsely claiming all the responsibility for the murder; the defense contended the notes backed up exactly what Bob had been saying from the very beginning, that it was all Roger's fault, that it was all an elaborate frame-up of Bob by his estranged older brother.

If it had been possible to get in Jennifer's testimony about the typed notes she'd sent to Bob without opening the door to the suicide notes, the prosecutors said later, they would have called Jennifer as a witness. But they couldn't find a way to do that without letting the jail suicide notes in.

"If we could have gotten it in, we would have put it in," Wilson said afterward. "But if we put it in, we'd've had to look at the suicide notes. See, we're fighting like hell to keep the suicide notes out. And when you look at what was said in those notes [from Roger via Jennifer to Bob], it talks about suicide, and that would open up the door, they could put in the suicide notes, and they would be able to say [that Roger said], 'My brother didn't do it.' ''

The prosecutors did not want to risk having the jury hear about the suicide notes because, they reasoned, it would simply confuse the jurors while giving them still more room for reasonable doubt about Bob's guilt.

Ironically, the positions were completely reversed for the rest of the evidence: The prosecutors wanted to show the contents of Roger's briefcase to the jury, including the video made of the microcasette tape transcription; the defense said *this* was hearsay, and so should be excluded.

And, of course, the arguments were exactly the reverse: Wilson and McClellan claimed the briefcase contents were admissible because they were statements 'Roger made against his own interest, and in the furtherance of a conspiracy; the defense asserted that the contents were not admissible because the state had never been able to prove who wrote the documents, when, or why.

The same point could be made about the notes from Jennifer found in Bob's closet; without Jennifer to testify that she had typed them at Roger's instructions, there was no way to authenticate them as a communication from Roger, the defense contended.

None of Bob's defense team had ever talked to Jennifer Manning, in any case.

"We sent J. J. Gradoni to talk to her," Schneider recalled, "but she refused to be interviewed."

One witness the defense hoped to procure for its side was Bob's mother, who was still living in New Jersey. Schneider said Mrs. Angleton was prepared to testify that Bob and Roger had never gotten along as children, and that Roger resented Bob as being the favorite child. She would testify that Roger and Bob often had physical altercations.

Indeed, Mrs. Angleton told Bob's lawyers that Roger had often communicated threats to Bob through her. On Mother's Day of 1997, in fact, Roger had called her and told her that he had killed Doris, and that he was going to get Bob or the girls next.

This was potentially powerful testimony for the defense—Roger's own mother saying her son was a murderous maniac. But Rains ruled the testimony inadmissible as irrelevant hearsay, particularly since Roger was no longer around to cross-examine.

As for the rest of the evidence, allowing the contents of the briefcase to be viewed or heard by the jury would be prejudicial to Bob's right to a fair trial, especially since "there [was] overwhelming evidence that none of the documents were authored" by Bob, Ramsey contended.

As for the Brothers Tape, the state had no way to prove it was Bob's voice, Ramsey argued, and in fact, had no way of knowing who made the tape, or where, or when. In the absence of any sort of authentication, the tape should not be heard by the jury, because it was simply too prejudicial.

Obviously, if the briefcase and the tape were thrown out, there was no case left.

Judge Brian Rains considered all these questions, and finally agreed, as the trial progressed, to keep even the fact that Roger had committed suicide out, along with the suicide notes, and to let the contents of the briefcase in, including the transcript of the pivotal tape.

As for Vanessa Leggett, although the prosecution subpoenaed her tapes, and copies were provided to the defense, the only way those tapes could be brought in was to have Vanessa testify, and that meant *everything* Roger had told Vanessa would be admissible, right down to the proverbial grassy knoll.

"We would have been in trial for weeks if all that stuff came in," Stan Schneider said afterward. As a result, neither side wanted anything to do with Vanessa's tapes of Roger's recollections.

By early July, as these legal maneuvers were still underway, Cain's report became public, including his assertion that eighty percent of the words on the exemplar and the Brothers Tape were very dissimilar.

"I think we now have conclusive evidence that Bob Angleton's voice is not on the tape, by an expert trusted by the state," Ramsey told the *Chronicle*'s Steve Brewer. "That's the state's case. There are other circumstances that look suspicious, but without the tape, there's no proof of anything."

And in an aside the following day, Ramsey cracked, "I wish the state would hire another expert."

THE TRIAL

TWENTY-NINE

The capital murder trial of Robert Nicholas Angleton opened on July 28. Brian Rains, the judge, warned both sides that he wanted to move as expeditiously as possible, and avoid getting bogged down in esoteric details. He limited both sides as to what evidence might be referred to in opening statements; given the case's notoriety in Houston, the last thing Rains wanted was an O. J. Simpson-style circus.

As it would turn out, the key witness for both sides was a television set.

McClellan opened for the prosecution by running through all the movements of Doris and Bob on the evening of the murder. Critical to those events, McClellan pointed out, was the issue of Ali's softball bat; it was Bob who left the bat behind, McClellan said.

In Texas, as in most jurisdictions, an opening statement is not an argument, but rather a review of the evidence that each side expects to put before the jury. McClellan prefaced all of his statements about the evidence with the words "I believe."

Methodically sketching in the basic events of what had happened, starting with Doris' desire to get a divorce, McClellan ended with discovery of the tape in Roger's briefcase.

"I believe the evidence will show that the recording is the voice of two males," McClellan said. "I believe the evidence will show it's the voice of Robert and Roger Angleton, plotting and planning the death of Doris Angleton.

"I believe the evidence will show that on that tape, not only through the identification of the voices, but from the words themselves, you will be able to determine that the voice . . . is that of Robert Angleton as well as Roger Angleton. I believe you will find evidence in that, [the] type of information only the homeowner should know, such as the alarm code to get in the house to disarm the alarm, 00032, the code to get in a gate that [gives] access to the driveway, 8184 asterisk."

McClellan detailed some of the other statements made by the voices on the tape, again suggesting that the words could only have come from someone intimately familiar with the house.

"Ultimately, I believe the evidence will show that, in addition to the tape, there's other evidence that will further corroborate the defendant's involvement in hiring his brother Roger Angleton, for remuneration, and the promise of remuneration, to take the life of Doris Angleton. I believe the evidence will show that Roger Angleton took her life with thirteen shots, all twenty-twos, but from two different weapons. I believe the evidence will show that he carried out that contract for murder."

Now it was Ramsey's turn.

"Ladies and gentlemen, here's what we expect to prove. Please treat everything I say as what I expect will be proved.

"Basically, it's as follows: Robert and Doris had been married for a period, a lengthy period of time. They had two, twin daughters. In February of 1997, Doris Angleton became disenchanted with the marriage, filed for a divorce. They did go into marriage counseling, and you will hear from the marriage counselor . . .

"For the benefit of the girls, they continued to live in the house. Bob Angleton was, in fact, very active with the girls . . . and was doing his best by counseling . . . to put the marriage back together."

Bob and Doris were amicably resolving their differences, Ramsey continued. Assets had been divided and arrangements had been worked out regarding child support and other such things.

"Now, one of the problems that existed—and you will hear about this as the case develops—is that one of Robert—Bob Angleton's, his principal profession, was that he was a bookmaker. He was a bookie. He catered to a clientele that lived in or near the neighborhood that he lived in . . .

"Many of his clients were doctors, lawyers, people of that sort. And he did that under the umbrella of the Houston Police Department because he was an informant, an enrolled informant, and had been for a period, a long period of time for the Houston Police Department. The officer who worked with him is an officer named Kevin Templeton . . . I believe the proof will show, who is on Governor Bush's crime task force.''

Ramsey was doing his best to take the sting out of the fact that Bob was a criminal by making his bookmaking seem both respectable, and even socially valuable to the police, maybe even to Governor Bush.

McClellan was wrong, Ramsey continued, when he claimed that the case began in early 1997. It actually went back to 1989, Ramsey said, when Bob "made the mistake" of hiring Roger to work in his bookmaking business.

"This case is a continuum from that day until now," Ramsey said. "Unless you understand the relationship between the two brothers, you will never understand the case as I view it."

Bob fired Roger, Ramsey said, "for a variety of reasons, dishonesty among them, misconduct in general among them, incompetence in general among them.

"And when he was fired, he reacted by setting up a blackmail of Mr. Bob Angleton. This took place in 1991. It was an extortion. It was a naked extortion."

Roger continually threatened Bob and Doris until Bob finally agreed to pay Roger to go away, Ramsey indicated. "A note was actually executed to pay Roger to basically stay away, stay shut up, and stay out of town.

"Now," Ramsey continued, "Roger Angleton at that period of time in his life, the proof will show, was in a serious, serious decline. To say that he was insane probably is to go a bit too far, but he was mentally deranged in a serious fashion. He was paranoid. He was threatening. He was essentially a man down on his luck who was making no money, or if he did make money, was making it by illegal means. Was on drugs.''

This was a tricky area; Ramsey had to simultaneously suggest that Roger was so desperate for money that he was willing to extort Bob to the point of murdering Doris, but somehow leave room to explain why Roger had more than $64,000 in his possession when he was arrested. ''Was on drugs'' was one possible way to do this, suggesting as it did that Roger's source of income was from the sale of drugs.

As a result of the first extortion, Ramsey continued, Doris had ''developed a cordial hatred for Roger, and I expect you will believe from the proof that it was returned.''

Roger suddenly came back to Houston in early 1997, Ramsey said; and he sent Bob ''an extremely threatening note. It said words to the effect, 'Pay me $200,000 in cash or I will hurt you in a way that will be with you for the rest of your life.'

''Now, Bob Angleton was in a position at that time where he had basically made up his mind. He had made enough money. He was in the process of getting out of the business, was not going to be subject to more blackmail and more extortion. And he knew he was dealing with a man who was essentially deranged. That is not to say he was not clever, guileful, deceitful.

''You will find that Roger was a person who was obsessed with guns. You will find that he was a person who was obsessed with all kinds of undercover disguise kind of activity, color[ing] his hair, ordering explosive bullets, doing all kinds of weird, really weird behavior. He was descending, in my mind, into this state of madness.''

McClellan rose to object.

''I object to what is in his [Ramsey's] mind,'' he said. ·

Ramsey said McClellan was correct to object, but that what he meant to say was that the jury would infer from the evidence that Roger was close to madness.

Ramsey took a swing at McClellan's suggestion that the softball bat was to be a lure to get Doris to the rear of the house.

He said the real reason Doris returned was to change her clothes.

''Both of the girls will testify in this case,'' Ramsey said. ''And both of them—one of them I think will say that she still bears guilt for this, that she said to her mother, 'That's the ugliest blouse you've got, Mom. Go home and change.' And Doris went home and to her death.''

Ramsey neared his time limit. He wanted to raise the two-shooter theory.

''I think the physical evidence will convince you there were not just one, but two shooters involved. There were two gunmen involved in the case.''

Ramsey continued.

''Now, I want you to understand this, that many of the writings of Roger Angleton, all of them that we can get into evidence—some of them are admissible, some are not—I believe will demonstrate that you are dealing with a man who is descending into the area of evil, that area of madness.

"This is a long-standing grudge. Bob should never have hired him. They never got along as children. They never got along as adults. Bob should never have hired him in 1989. That's the decision for which Mr. Angleton is guilty. That's what Bob Angleton did wrong, was to hire a brother who was an evil man."

After mentioning the expectation of voice identification evidence, Ramsey tried to address something McClellan had not brought up in his opening statement.

"If, in fact, he was hiding cash or did not want to split up cash or not want to surface cash because of IRS problems, the most certain way in the world to have that happen would be to cause the death of a wife he still loved."

"Your Honor, I object," McClellan said. "That's not anticipating what the evidence will show." It was more in the line of argument than outlining the evidence, McClellan was suggesting.

"I anticipate the evidence will show that, Your Honor," said Ramsey. "That he was familiar intimately with police procedure, and the jury can infer from what we will prove, that essentially, there is no motive whatsoever, if you look at that case closely.

"That, in fact, Bob Angleton, according to the testimony of the marriage counselor, was trying very desperately to make the marriage work, still living in the same house with his wife and his two beloved daughters."

The import of this was that the very last thing Bob

would have done, if faced with possible trouble from the IRS, was to have Doris killed, because that only would have brought attention to Bob.

"And with that, Your Honor, I will close," Ramsey concluded.

THIRTY

Now came the laborious task of bringing the actual evidence before the jury. Because the case against Bob, with the exception of the tape found in Roger's briefcase, was entirely circumstantial, it required thoughtful planning on both sides.

"The hardest part was trying to visualize in your mind how to put this thing on, how to structure it," McClellan said later. "Where to start, what to put first, second, third. And I was real uncomfortable with the case until finally Ted and I sat down and figured out exactly how we were going to present the evidence. You can't just say, well, we're going to prove this. Well, *how* are we going to prove this?"

McClellan and Wilson began with a neighbor who had seen Doris arrive around 6:30 P.M., and who said he had seen or heard nothing else until the police arrived about 9:45. That testimony seemed to suggest that whoever had shot Doris, he or she had been in the house prior to Doris' arrival.

The tape from Bob's call to 911 was played, and then Officer Carr came on to tell of his discovery of the body. Carr told the jury about Bob's initial re- action to Carr's discovery of Doris' body, and that

Bob had wanted him to tell the girls about the murder.

Now the state went into the details of the murder scene, calling Brian Foster and crime scene technician Leroy Tuttle to testify about the location of the body and the bullet holes in the walls, as well as the fact that the house had apparently not been burgled.

Now came an important witness, Dr. Brown, the assistant medical examiner. On the second day of the trial, Brown testified as to the shots that had hit Doris, indicating that Doris was still alive when the last shots were fired into her brain.

But on cross-examination, Schneider was able to get Brown to acknowledge that it was possible that Doris had been fired on from two different directions, thus bolstering the defense's contention that two shooters might have been involved. The obvious inference Schneider hoped the jury would draw was that the second shooter—who couldn't have been Bob, who was at the game—was Voice Number Two on the tape.

In turn, this would dovetail with suggestions that the police themselves had uncovered that Roger had been seen around Houston with a younger, athletic man—presumably, the legendary ''second shooter.''

After some ballistics testimony, in which an expert held that two different .22-caliber weapons were used in shooting Doris, the prosecutors called Detective Wright. Wright told the jury about his interview with Bob, and said that Bob had never mentioned Roger to him the night of the murder. With Wright on the stand, the prosecutors were now able to play the tape

of Wright's interview with Bob. That was twice that
the state had taken the opportunity to expose the jury
to the sound and cadence of Bob's voice, preparation
for the eventual playing of the Brothers Tape.

After using an assistant district attorney from San
Diego to establish that Roger was wanted for failing
to appear on his drug charges in that state, the prosecutors now called one of their most important witnesses, Kevin Templeton, Bob's control with the vice
squad. The state wanted to use Templeton to show
the circumstances under which Bob had given Roger
as a suspect to the the homicide detectives.

Templeton at first seemed a bit nervous under Wilson's questioning.

Templeton told the jury that he first heard of Doris'
murder when he got a telephone call from a retired
former sergeant of the vice squad, Stan Plaster, who
told him to turn on the television on the morning of
April 17. After seeing that Doris had been murdered,
Templeton immediately called a sergeant in the homicide unit and asked to speak to the homicide investigators handling the Angleton case.

"Did you provide any information . . . in that initial conversation?" Wilson asked.

"I did," Templeton said. "I told him that there
was a sensitive matter involving this situation, and
that I needed to discuss it with the investigators, because of Mr. Angleton's position as an informant."

The homicide sergeant said he would pass the message on, but investigators Wright and Foster didn't
call him back. Eventually he passed the information
about Bob on to Lieutenant Nelson Zoch, the homi-

cide supervisor. Shortly thereafter, he received a call from George Tyson, Bob's lawyer, asking him to come to Tyson's office.

"Now," said Wilson, "prior to April 16, 1997, did this defendant ever show you any note purportedly written to him by Roger Angleton prior to the sixteenth, prior to the death of Doris Angleton?"

"No, sir," Templeton said.

When he arrived at Tyson's office, Bob was already there, Templeton said. Tyson then gave him the letter from Roger, the one in which Roger had threatened to come to Houston and "make you pay dearly."

"Was that the first time you ever saw that?"

"Yes, sir, it was."

Wilson asked Templeton if he'd been in regular contact with Bob throughout March, and Templeton said he had been; the implication was that Bob had had ample opportunity to pass the note over to Templeton before Doris' murder, but hadn't done so.

"Okay," said Wilson. "When you saw that note, what did you do then?"

"I told Mr. Tyson that we were going to need to stop this conversation, that I needed to call homicide, and I notified homicide from the scene, from the office right there."

"Why would you want to call homicide?"

"Because I was presented with crucial evidence involving a murder case," Templeton said.

Templeton said that when Novak told him to come in with the note, he took the note first to his own sergeant in vice, and then the two went to see Novak,

Ferguson, and Zoch in the homicide office, where he passed the note over to the detectives.

After a brief recess, it was Tyson's turn to question Templeton. Templeton seemed more comfortable with Tyson than he had with Wilson.

"Officer Templeton, I'm George Tyson. And you and I have met, have we not?"

"Yes, sir, we have."

"We met a long time ago, or several years ago?"

"Yes, it was."

"Tell the jury when you and I met, and what the circumstances were."

Templeton said he'd first met Tyson in 1992, when Bob's voice had been picked up on a federal wiretap of another bookmaker. The FBI wanted Templeton to identify a voice they did not recognize, who turned out to be Bob.

Templeton then explained to the FBI that Bob was his informant, and that the reason the FBI had picked up Bob on their wiretap was because the Houston police were investigating the same bookmaker as the federal government. Until Templeton identified Bob and claimed him as an informant, the FBI knew nothing about Bob's book, even though it was one of the largest in the county.

After some discussion of Bob's role in the federal case, Tyson asked Templeton to tell the jury what a "problem informant" was.

"Okay," said Templeton. "The department policy does allow us to use problem informants. Problem informant, again, is anybody that's continued, continuing to engage in criminal activity, which Mr. An-

gleton was doing at the time he was an informant
with the police department. He was involved in the
gambling community, the Houston-Harris County,
and the Texas area.''

"And at your request, was he not? I mean, you
wanted him to give you information about bookmaking activities, correct?''

"That's correct.''

"And you can't do that with a fellow that's not in
the bookmaking business, can you?''

"Plain and simple,'' Templeton agreed. "That's
the way I define it. It is the nature of the beast and—
you know, the Pope and the bishops and the mayors
and the governors don't give us information on gambling activity. It's the people that are involved in the
gambling activity that we have to rely upon to learn
what's going on.''

Tyson wanted to establish the idea that even if he
was breaking the law in gambling, Bob was doing it
for the forces of good.

"Problem informant doesn't mean they're a problem,'' he said. "It means there is a potential there for
activity since the nature of their work requires them
to keep—to keep on doing what they're doing?''

"That's true,'' Templeton agreed.

"And Mr. Angleton did keep on doing what he
was doing, didn't he?''

"As far as the gambling?''

"Yes.''

"Yes, sir.''

"And did it well, did he not?''

"I would say he did it very well.''

After establishing that Bob had consistently provided reliable information about other bookmakers that resulted in arrests and seizures, Tyson turned to the subject of the note he had given Templeton on April 17.

"And did I call you and ask you to come to the office, in the morning?"

Templeton said that was true.

"Describe to the jury Mr. Angleton's demeanor when you saw him."

"Uh," Templeton said. "He was upset. He was—seated in the couch, kind of slumped over, relaxed in the couch. His eyes were reddened and swollen, and it looked like he'd obviously been up all evening. He looked upset and concerned."

"Did that strike you as unusual for a man who had just lost his wife and—"

"It's what I expected," Templeton said.

Tyson gave Templeton the first note from Roger, about making him "pay dearly."

"When you read that document I handed you, did you deem it of importance?"

"Yes, I did."

"Did you try to communicate the importance of the document to homicide by telephone?"

"Yes, I did."

"How was your calling to homicide received, in your opinion?"

"Not very well," Templeton said. The homicide people were "not at all pleased" to learn of his relationship with Bob, he said.

Tyson now tried to show that the homicide detectives from the beginning had treated Bob shabbily and suspiciously.

"Were you concerned as the investigation went on—and I'm talking about the way you handled your business—were you concerned as a vice officer about leaks relative to informants in this case getting into the newspaper?"

"I was very concerned," Templeton said.

"Were there a series of leaks out of this case of information, to your knowledge, known only to police?"

"Yes, there were."

"And did that even go so far as to identify Mr. Angleton to the world as a confidential informant?"

"Yes."

"Were his concerns about that legitimate, in your opinion?"

"I would be very concerned if I was him, having my name put in the paper like that," Templeton said.

Now Tyson tried to mitigate Templeton's earlier testimony about Bob's failure to provide the note before Doris' murder. He wanted to establish that Bob had told Templeton long before the murder that he was afraid of Roger. Wilson vigorously objected, and the judge agreed that Templeton could not say *what* Bob had said, only whether he had reported Bob's prior statements to the homicide detectives on April 17.

Templeton said he had, indeed, told the detectives that Bob had been worried about Roger for some time. This helped mitigate the fact that Bob hadn't turned the note over to Templeton as soon as he received it, and underscored the idea that Bob had for some time been concerned about threats from Roger.

THIRTY-ONE

' Throughout the next few days, the prosecution continued bringing in witnesses, using their testimony as a framework for various identifications of Roger, trying to develop a pattern of movements establishing that Roger had been in Houston at the time of the murder. In effect, the prosecutors had to try a dead man for the crime, and show the motives for his actions.

This soon led to the episode at the Dallas-Fort Worth airport, and Roger's identification as the man with guns in the suitcase at the airport.

While this allowed the prosecution to tenuously link Roger to the events of the murder, it gave the defense a chance to thoroughly characterize Roger as a very squirrelly person, one given to disguises, false indentifications, addicted to painkillers; the notes about Doris' schedule, combined with the binoculars placed into evidence by the defense, helped the defense create the impression that Roger had been stalking Doris for some time.

From the suitcase, the prosecution went on to the briefcase, calling Shani Coleman, the Las Vegas hotel clerk, to describe how Roger had first attracted her attention with his phony driver's license. Then came a witness from the Las Vegas police, who told of seizing Roger's briefcase; that set the stage for the introduction of all of the various typewritten and handwritten notes found in the briefcase, as well as the now-infamous tape.

To bring the materials into the case, the prosecution called Jerry Novak.

While all this material had to be introduced to buttress the prosecution's theory—that Roger had executed a contract with Bob, and that the writings were evidence of the contract—it also provided the defense with an opportunity to portray Roger as crazy. This solved a real problem for the defense, because, with Novak testifying as to all of Roger's antics, there was now no need to put Bob on the stand to get the information from him.

"Novak was our best witness," defense lawyer Stan Schneider said later. "Because of him, we didn't have to put Bob on the stand. Novak gave us everything we wanted the jury to hear about Roger." That included information about the 1991 extortion attempt, as well as the draft vendetta letters, which the state had chosen not to introduce.

Under the questioning from the defense, Novak was on the stand for more than five hours, spread out over three days.

Then it was time for the state's star witness: the tape.

Using the videotape prepared earlier by the police lab, the prosecution ran the words and sound of Voices Number One and Two. The jury listened to the tape in its entirety, including the various references to "Roger," "my house," the planning for the murder, and all the discussion about the alarm system and the motion detectors, the ring, the dog, and the doors.

After the tape was played, Novak was recalled to the witness stand. Wilson asked him if he had identified Voice Number Two as Bob. Novak said that he had.

Schneider, on his cross-examination, suggested to Novak that it was possible that Roger, while in Las Vegas, had hired an impressionist to mimic Bob.

That prompted Wilson to sarcastically ask Novak if he and Ferguson had taken any statements from Rich Little when they were in Las Vegas, which prompted Rains to chide Wilson for beginning his closing argument too soon.

After Novak came a stream of people who knew Doris well and who had social dealings with Bob, mostly through the Briar Club. Also called was Bill Beck, Doris' first husband. Beck said he had listened to the tape and was convinced that Voice Number Two was Bob. But on cross-examination, Beck acknowledged that he didn't like Bob, and that he thought from the start that Bob was involved in the murder.

Worse for the prosecution, Bob's defense was able to establish that most of these witnesses had been surrounded by others, including Detectives Ferguson and Novak, when the tape was played; even Ferguson acknowledged that the correct procedure would have been for the witnesses to listen to the tape alone, so their judgment could not be influenced by others.

The state now recalled Kevin Templeton to identify the voice, having earlier established that Templeton had frequently talked to Bob both over the telephone and in person.

"When you listened to [the tape], were you able to recognize the voice of one of the individuals . . . on the tape?" Wilson asked.

"Yes, I do," Templeton said.

"Whose voice do you recognize?"

"I recognize the voice of Robert Angleton."

This seemed simple enough, but Tyson was prepared to try to poke holes in Templeton's testimony.

"Officer Templeton," Tyson said, "when you listened to the tape the first time, you gave a qualified opinion, didn't you?"

"Qualified opinion the first time I listened to it?"

"Yeah," Tyson said. "You said you couldn't tell [from] the first twenty minutes whether Bob was on the tape, didn't you?"

"Well," Templeton said, "it took me a while to make a decision, yes, that's correct."

Tyson had planted a seed, and would soon return to harvest it.

"Of course, had Bob Angleton had anything to do with the death of Doris Angleton, that would be inconsistent with what you knew about the person who had served as your informant and had provided so much truthful information in the past, and so on, correct?"

"Correct," Templeton said.

"And let's tell the jury about the circumstances, your own personal circumstances vis-à-vis the police department [when] you listened to the tape recording, okay?"

Tyson went on to establish that although Templeton was probably the one person in the police department who was most familiar with Bob's voice, the homicide investigators had not asked him to listen to the tape until June, just before the trial began. Even then, he listened to it under the gaze of assistant district attorneys Wilson and McClellan.

"Were you anxious—I'm talking about your state of mind—were you anxious that you had not been asked to listen to the tape up to that point?"

"It did go through my mind, yes," Templeton said.

"You felt like you had been in trouble with the department ever since the arrest, did you not, sir?"

Wilson objected, and Templeton was not permitted to answer.

Tyson tried another way.

"Well, during this time period, isn't it true that there was an internal affairs investigation—"

Wilson objected again, and again Templeton was prevented from answering.

Now followed a series of questions from Tyson, in which he attempted to get Templeton to say that at the time he first listened to the tape, he was under a cloud from the department, and that suggestions had been made by the district attorney's office that if he didn't identify Bob on the tape, things would go badly for him on his job.

But the judge wasn't having any of this and kept sustaining Wilson's objections.

Tyson then caused Templeton to admit it was only after hearing the tape for a third time that Templeton felt ready to testify that it was Bob's voice.

Tyson honed in on what he was trying to cast as improper pressure from the prosecution on Templeton.

"Since you testified on Wednesday, has the prosecutor's office made it clear to you, with contact with your attorney, that they were dissatisfied—"

Wilson made another objection.

The judge sent the jury out of the room, then asked Tyson what grounds he had to ask the question about pressure being brought on Templeton by the prosecutors.

"For the state of mind of this witness, in terms of what he needs to do to save his job," Tyson said. "He is—the proof will be, Your Honor, that he has been pressured about the testimony that he gave and the testimony that he's given, and that's what I'm trying to prove to the jury."

The judge turned to Wilson.

"I'm curious as to how the district attorney's office would somehow threaten a witness in a case," the judge said.

"I didn't threaten the witness," Wilson said. "His lawyer called me and asked me how he did. I said he appeared to be very nervous on the stand . . . and that he seemed to be more comfortable when he was on cross-examination. That's the extent of it. I don't think that was a threat in any form or fashion."

Templeton was now asked if anyone had said anything to him about the internal investigation while he was listening to the tape. Templeton said McClellan had suggested to him that the internal affairs investigation wasn't over until he testified about the tape.

"It's not admissible and won't be allowed," Judge Rains ruled.

The jury was returned, and Tyson once more set about trying to shake Templeton's identification of Bob as Voice Number Two.

"And you had a doubt, didn't you?" Tyson asked Templeton.

"The first time, yes," Templeton said.

"All right," Tyson said, "and you could be mistaken, couldn't you, sir? Anything is possible, isn't it?"

Templeton nodded yes, anything was possible.

"And you could be mistaken, couldn't you, sir?"

"Possibly."

Now Tyson had inflicted some damage on the state's one witness who was most familiar with the sound of Bob's voice. Wilson had to try to rehabilitate him.

"The bottom line is, you look at this jury, and your opinion, is that Bob Angleton?" Wilson asked.

"My opinion is that it is Bob Angleton on the tape," Templeton said.

Tyson had one more volley. It had been more than sixteen months since Templeton had talked to Bob, wasn't that true? Templeton said it was.

THIRTY-TWO

After Templeton left the stand, Wilson and McClellan called a number of other witnesses who knew Bob, and who had also listened to the tape; these included friends of Doris', as well as a Bellaire police officer who knew Bob, and an FBI agent who had worked with Bob on a bookmaking case. All said that they believed it was Bob's voice on the tape; the FBI agent produced the 1992 wiretape tape with Bob's voice on it, and this was played. Now the jury had heard three other examples of Bob's voice, not counting the tape that was in dispute.

Next the state brought in an expert on the Ella Lee alarm system, who testified that the discussion of the system on the tape corresponded with the features found in the system installed in the Angleton house; he was followed by a police constable who had responded to the alarm when it was triggered on April 10, which seemed to validate the tape's discussion of the first, aborted attempt on Doris' life.

Doris' divorce lawyer, Tom Conner, was called to testify as to the freezing of the safe-deposit boxes, and to the fact that he had referred Doris to the tax lawyer Ed Urquhart. After this came witnesses who testified as to Bob's various safe-deposit boxes, winding up with Ferguson, who told of his seizure of the $3.4 million from the various banks over the previous year.

Finally, Wilson and McClellan called the Houston

Police Department's fingerprint expert, Debbie Ben-ningfield, who told the jury that she had identified Bob's fingerprints on the money wrapper found in Roger's briefcase.

The state rested its case.

The defense now began its side, and it went directly to the heart of the state's evidence—the tape.

After introducing the exemplar tape into evidence, Bob's team cued up their own videotape—this one of voice identification expert Steve Cain, the man originally hired by Wilson. Because Cain was unable to be present, the defense was permitted to use a videotape of his testimony that had been made on July 24.

Cain testified that he'd originally been asked by Wilson to do three things: Determine whether the Brothers Tape had been edited by anyone; determine if the casette the detectives had found was an original or a copy; and to enhance the tape so the words might be made clearer.

Cain said he'd been able to determine that the tape had not been edited, because there were no telltale marks on the tape showing the recorder being shut on and off, as one might expect if it were doctored. He couldn't tell if the tape was an original or a copy, because he hadn't been sent the original tape re-corder. He was able to determine that the tape re-corder seized from Roger's suitcase was *not* the recorder used to make the tape.

After he'd reported this to Novak, Cain said, he was asked to determine whether the voice on the tape was that of Bob. To do this, Bob had to provide the exemplar.

Asked if he had seen any evidence of faking by Bob in the exemplar, Cain said he had not.

"In your opinion, sir, had Mr. Angleton complied with the instructions that you transmitted to the district attorney's office?" Ramsey asked.

"Yes, he did," Cain said.

When he got the exemplar, Cain continued, he ran a spectroscopic analysis of the exemplar and compared it to similar phrases and words on the Brothers Tape. Cain said he'd run at least a hundred such tests. The tests provided a visual picture of the voices, which were run through a computer, and then printed in the form of a series of charts.

The charts showed the voices were "spectrographically dissimilar almost consistently throughout," Cain said. Among these phrases were the words, "She caught you by surprise," "It may get hung up," and "Now what you need to do is rewrite this."

Cain was asked what he'd told the district attorney's office about his analysis.

"I told them that the examination showed enough dissimilarities between the questioned voice and the voice on the exemplar that I would render an opinion of a possible elimination of Mr. Robert Angleton as the unknown speaker in this case," Cain said.

After Cain's videotape was played, Bob's side called another voice identification expert, Lonnie Smrkovski; Smrkovski, a former Michigan police officer, had trained Cain in voice analysis. He said he, too, tested the tape and the exemplar, at Tyson's request, and agreed with Cain's conclusions, that the voice on the tape was not Bob.

That was it, the experts had spoken. Now it would be up to others, chiefly Niki and Ali, to back up this opinion with their own.

Ramsey called a parade of witnesses, people who knew Bob, including Tommy and Julie Hughes, who said that it wasn't Bob's voice on the tape.

Among these people was Dr. Ann Moon, the marriage counselor who had been working with Doris and Bob. Moon said she'd been seeing Doris sporadically since 1989, for a total of nearly ninety sessions, about a third of which Bob had also attended. She testified that the Bob Angleton she knew was incapable of violence, and particularly arranging the murder of Doris. She agreed that the voice on the tape was not Bob's. She added that Novak had called for an appointment to interview her about Doris and Bob, but then hadn't bothered to show up.

After testimony from the former deputy district attorney who had represented Bob in his 1991 dispute with Roger, the defense called J. J. Gradoni, the private detective, who told of searching for Roger in the days immediately after the murder; the implication was, if Bob had been up to his neck with Roger in a plot to kill Doris, why would he attempt to wreck his plan by sending Gradoni after him? Both men also said the voice on the tape was not Bob's.

Now the stage was set for Ali and Niki.

THIRTY-THREE

As Ali took the witness stand, there wasn't a person in the courtroom who didn't feel for her. First her mother had been brutally murdered, then her father was accused of the crime, and finally, her uncle, the one man who could clear her father by admitting his own guilt, had committed suicide. Now she was being asked to try to save her father from the possibility of lethal injection. It had been a rough year for Ali and her sister, there was no question about that.

Tyson's task was to get Ali through her testimony without making it seem that he was using her for any mawkish purposes; that might backfire with the jury. On the other hand, he wanted to impress the jury with Ali's attractive sincerity and her clear love for her father.

Tyson first had Ali identify herself, and then took her through a series of simple questions about herself, and her sister.

"You just had a birthday?"

"Yes, sir."

"And now you're fourteen?"

"Yes."

"Now, your dad was arrested last year. Do you remember what day he was arrested?"

"August first, my birthday," Ali said.

"Okay. And since then, where have you lived?"

"With the Welshes."

This was a nice effort by Tyson to remind the jury that not only had the girls' father been taken away from them by the state, it had happened on their birthday. By bringing up the Welshes, Tyson was sending the clear message that if the jury convicted Bob, the girls, for all practical purposes, would be orphans.

Tyson had Ali describe the last time she'd seen her uncle Roger, and then veered into the subject of codes. Ali said that Bob's lucky number was 32, and it was used for the burglar alarm system even when the family had lived in Bellaire when she was a little girl. Since Roger was a frequent visitor to the Bellaire house, it was therefore likely that Roger knew about Bob's lucky number and his code.

After a few more questions, Tyson went to the crime itself.

"Ali, let's go to April sixteenth. Now, that's the day your mom died, okay?"

Ali nodded.

"Are you ready?"

"Uh-huh."

After a few questions about the day's schedule of softball games, Tyson asked if Ali had had a very good day batting, and she said that she had not. As a result, Bob removed her bat from the car and helped her with her swing in the backyard batting cage. Afterward, Ali went in to eat dinner with Niki and Doris.

Tyson now digressed, temporarily.

"Up until that time, as far as you knew, had your mom and dad been getting along okay?"

"Uh, not really."

"Okay. When did you first realize they were having some problems?"

"Uh, about a month, a month or two before."

"Would you tell the jury how you found that out?"

"When my parents took us out to eat at Ninfa's, and they just talked to us about it."

"You and your sister and your mom and your dad, correct?"

"Yes, sir."

"And were you surprised?"

"Yes, sir."

"And were you upset?"

"Yes, sir."

But after the initial discussion, it seemed to Ali that Bob and Doris had been getting along better.

Ali now testified as to the events just before the game, how Doris brought her and Niki to the field in time for batting practice. Now Ali added some information that undercut the prosecution's theory of the bat as a lure.

"So," Tyson said, "did your mom always stay through batting practice and wait for the game to begin?"

"Never," Ali said.

"Do the other moms ever stay for batting practice and wait for the game to begin?"

"No, sir."

"They always leave, don't they?" Tyson asked.

"Yes, sir."

If the mothers never stayed for batting practice, there would be no need to leave the bat behind as a lure, Tyson's question implied; Doris would be going home anyway.

When Doris dropped them off, Ali said, Doris told them she was going back to change clothes. That was when she, Ali, not Bob, remembered the bat, and asked her mother to pick it up, Ali said.

If Tyson had to be careful with Ali, Wilson had to treat her as if she were nitroglycerine. If the jury so much as got a single whiff of aggression by Wilson toward the twins, they were almost certain to vote to acquit just out of spite toward the state.

"Ali," he began, and then corrected himself. "May I call you Ali?"

"Yes, sir."

Wilson gently reminded Ali that the last time he had spoken to her was at the grand jury hearing; Ali remembered this was so.

"Ali, I don't want to ask you a lot of questions," Wilson said. "I know this is difficult, but do you remember when you were in the grand jury that I asked you about your father asking your mother to go back and get the bat? Do you remember that?"

"Yes, sir."

"Do you remember what you told the grand jury?"

"No, sir."

Wilson now gave Ali a copy of her grand jury testimony, and asked her to read it.

"Now, do you remember what you told the grand jury, Ali?"

"I told them that my dad was asking my mom if

she could go back when she went back and pick up the bat.''

"That it was your father [who] asked your mother to go back home and get the bat?''

"Uh-huh.''

After more discussion about the bat, including an inconclusive exchange over who had placed the bat on the deck, Wilson moved on to the subject of Bob's cellular phones, and raising the question of why Bob hadn't simply called Doris before she left to remind her to bring the bat.

"Okay,'' said Wilson, "while you, your sister, and your mom were home, did your dad ever call to mention anything about the bat?''

"I don't remember.''

Despite his initial determination to appear benign with Ali, Wilson was becoming increasingly aggressive.

"You had phones in your house, of course, right?''
"Yes.''

"Did she have a cell phone also, Ali?''

"Yes, but she didn't have it on all the time,'' Ali said. Wilson had succeeded in making Ali look defensive, even if it was probably hurting him with the jury.

After more questions about Bob's attempts to call Doris during the game, Wilson came to the events when the body was discovered.

"Did your dad try to get out of the Blazer and go in and try to help your mom?''

"Well, we didn't want him to go inside.''

Wilson kept pressing the point, with his questions,

that Bob hadn't gone inside to see if Doris was all right. He made the point, through questions to Ali, that even when Tex arrived, Bob and Tex still did not enter the house.

Wilson's cross-examination of Ali actually accomplished very little; even in getting her to admit that her testimony had changed over the bat issue, he'd only made people feel sorry for her, and by extension, Bob.

Tyson now took Ali back as a witness.

"Now," he said, "I want to ask you another question. Did I ask you to listen to a tape recording that was pretty lengthy, about forty-five minutes, and had two unidentified men speakers on it? Do you remember me asking you to do that?"

"Yes, sir."

"Did you do that?"

"Yes, sir."

"Did I ask you after you listened to it if you recognized your dad's voice on the tape recording?"

"Yes, sir."

"And did you recognize your dad's voice on the tape recording?"

"No, sir."

"Was his voice on the tape recording?"

"No, sir."

Niki now followed her sister to the witness stand, and told pretty much the same story. In Niki's memory, however, Bob had asked Doris to bring the bat back with her; she agreed with her sister that Doris had gone home to change clothes.

When they arrived at the house after the game, Niki said, she was the one who first noticed that the back door was open.

"Was there any discussion about him [Bob] going in[to] the house?"

"Yes."

"Were you all involved in that discussion?"

"Yes."

"And did you—what did you tell him?"

"We told him we did not want him going inside because we were scared that someone might come outside and hurt us or something."

"You didn't know where your mom was?"

"No. We had no clue."

"And you didn't know if anybody was in the house, did you?"

"No."

After asking Niki some of the same questions he'd asked Ali, about the codes and the combinations to the alarm and the safe, Tyson took up the subject of how they first learned that their mother was dead.

"Now, after Tex took you home, later on, did you know what was going on?"

"No."

"Did your dad come in and talk to you?"

"Yeah."

"And did he tell you about your mom?"

"Yeah."

"And he was pretty upset?"

"Yes."

"Did you see him later that evening?"

"Yeah."

"Tell the jury about that."

"Uh, me and my sister were in my friend Katherine's room at the Welshes' house, and he—he came in. He opened the door and asked Katherine to leave, and we could tell by his face, already. And he came, and we sat on the bed, and we started crying. He didn't have to say anything."

After a pause for effect, Tyson resumed.

"Did I ask you to listen to a tape recording of two men that lasted about forty-five minutes, Niki?"

"Yes."

"Did I ask you to do that last week?"

"Yes."

"Did I ask you to listen to the tape last week?"

Niki began to cry.

"Did you do that?"

"Yes, sir."

"Did I ask you if you recognized your father's voice on the tape?"

"Yes."

"Did you recognize his voice?"

"No, sir."

"Is he on the tape?"

"No."

There was almost nothing Wilson could do on cross-examination with this testimony. He tried to reiterate with questions to Niki that Bob hadn't gone into the house to look to see where Doris was, but it did not seem that his heart was in it.

"Niki, I don't have any other questions," Wilson said. "We're awfully sorry about your mom, okay?"

But Tyson wasn't finished with Niki.

"Do you have a dog?"

"Yes."

"What's the dog's name?"

"Dasher."

"Okay. Is Dasher pretty smart?"

"Dasher is very smart."

"If you put Dasher in the laundry room and shut the door, will Dasher stay in there?"

"No."

"Why not?"

"She can open it, real easily."

"And does she do it all the time?"

"All the time."

"Everybody in your family know that?"

"Yeah."

"Have you ever heard your dad use the term 'foyer'?"

"No."

"Ever?"

"No."

"Now, the back room of the house, where the pool table is—"

"Uh-huh."

"Did he call that the library?"

"No."

"What did he call that?"

"The game room."

"What do you-all call the little room in the front?"

"The library."

"Did you sometimes call it the green room?"

"No."

Now Tyson had elicited a series of answers from

Niki that indicated whoever the man on the tape had been, it wasn't Bob Angleton, who certainly knew that the dog could get out of the washroom, who knew the "back library" was called the game room, who knew the library in front was never called the green room.

It wasn't Bob on the tape, Tyson's questions said.

THIRTY-FOUR

Both Niki and Ali emerged as extraordinarily effective witnesses; coupled with the voice experts' testimony about the tape, it appeared that the state's case against Bob was ending in a whimper.

It would be up to Wilson and McClellan to put some pep back into it in their closing arguments. But the state waived its right to go first; McClellan said later they wanted to hear Ramsey give Bob's side first so they could decide how to attack.

This put Ramsey at a slight disadvantage, in that if he failed to cover some telling point in his summation, the prosecution could draw the jury's attention to its omission.

Ramsey tried to cover this contingency by telling the jury, "[I] will ask this favor of you—remembering that I can't respond when the state argues—ask yourself: What would Ramsey have said if he had the chance? That's only fair."

It seemed clear to him, Ramsey said, that the case against Bob Angleton broke into a number of components: the tape; the history of Doris and Bob with

Roger; the character of Roger; the theory of the two gunmen; and finally, the overall view of what had really happened to Bob and Doris Angleton.

One of the most remarkable things about the whole case, Ramsey said, was the utter absence of evidence that Roger even did the shooting.

"Now," he said, "I believe that Roger did the shooting; I'm not going to argue to you that he did not. He and a cohort did. [But] when you start to look at *proof,* it's not in the case even, which is remarkable, to my mind, in a capital murder prosecution."

The entire case against Bob revolved around the tape, Ramsey said.

"By a preponderance of evidence or any way you want to test it, we have demonstrated to you that Bob Angleton's voice is not on that tape."

There were four ways to analyze the tape, Ramsey said: the witnesses who knew Bob and who listened to the tape for either the prosecution or the defense; the experts who had tried to analyze it scientifically; the meaning of the words spoken on the tape; and the comparison of the voice on the tape to the other tapes in which Bob's voice was known to be included, such as the 911 tape, the interview with Mike Wright, the FBI tape, and the voice exemplar.

Ramsey said that as far as he could see, the witnesses who said it was not Bob's voice on the tape were more believable than those who said it was.

Recalling Ali and Niki's testimony, Ramsey pointed out that the tape was purported to be a conspiracy between Roger and Bob to murder the twins' mother.

"Do you think those girls would listen to that tape, do you think Bob would have permitted them to be exposed to the tape, or I would have permitted them to be exposed to the tape, if they were going to find their dad's voice on it? No."

Even Dr. Moon, a professional psychotherapist, was convinced it wasn't Bob on the tape, Ramsey said.

"Sergeant Novak made an appointment [with Dr. Moon] one time, but never followed up on it," Ramsey said. "Don't you think the police ought to have at least been interested if the separation was cordial? They were still living in the same room.

"What advice do you think that woman [Moon] would have given them if she saw any hint of danger on the horizon? What advice do you think she would have given Doris, who was her primary client?" The fact that Doris hadn't moved out of the house, or got a court order to have Bob removed from the house demonstrated that Doris had no fear of Bob.

Having built up his own witnesses, Ramsey now tried to knock the prosecution's down.

"The Briar Club ladies," Ramsey said, referring to Doris' friends who believed it was Bob on the tape. "You might say the Nancy Drew division of the Briar Club. [They] get together at Mary Hill's house. Have Sergeant Ferguson and Sergeant Novak come over after they know from the newspapers that there's a tape recording that's supposed to have Bob Angleton's voice on it. And [they] listen to it in a group, after they've been laying around, cutting it up among themselves for months, and deciding among themselves that Bob Angleton must be guilty in the case.''

That wasn't proper police procedure, Ramsey said. Even Ferguson admitted that.

''The way you are supposed to do it is the way we did it,'' Ramsey said, in which most of the defense witnesses listened to the tape alone.

''An even better way, the police should do, since they're set up to do it, is like an ear lineup . . . to let them listen to five or six samples—and they had five or six samples—to see whether or not they could identify Bob Angleton's voice.''

Ramsey wondered where the Briar Club ladies' husbands were, while they were busy deciding that Bob was guilty. Why hadn't *they* testified that it was Bob?

''These women had too much time on their hands, too much money in their pockets, and stayed around the Briar Club, tried the case among themselves, and decided to convict Bob. Well, that's *your* job. That's not *their* job.''

Now let's get to the experts, Ramsey said.

The experts agreed, Ramsey said, even Cain, who was originally hired by the state—the voice on the tape was significantly different from that of Bob.

''The reason they can't get stronger [in eliminating Bob] is because the original tape is a degraded quality . . . but that, in and of itself, from people as respected as they are in their profession, has got to be the kind of thing that makes people hesitate to act.'' It was, Ramsey thus suggested, reasonable doubt.

And what about the words used on the tape? Ramsey asked.

"We don't know where it was made. We don't know how this was made. We don't know when it was made. We don't know whose voices are on it, but there are words that give you clues.

"*Garage*, for example, was used clearly. You can hear that word. There's no garage on this house, it's a carport. *Foyer* is used. The girls both testified that Bob never used that word."

There were other hints, Ramsey said. There was a reference to a daughter being ill, but no records were ever introduced to show that either Niki or Ali were sick during the time in question. Ramsey cited several other examples of inconsistencies between the Ella Lee house and the house discussed on the tape.

As for the alarm, "It's obviously two people who are talking about a burglar alarm system, and it sounds like talk between two idiots. They're obviously looking at a book. Listen to the tape and you will hear this . . .

"But these people are like idiots," Ramsey continued. "They're reading to each other for on and on and on, trying to explain how to use a burglar alarm that both of the people that testified about burglar alarms say they can teach you how to use in twenty seconds. That's—that's just absurd. It is a total absurdity."

The fact that Bob had worked as a bookmaker for years may have in fact prompted the charges against him, Ramsey suggested.

"Now, they were dealing with what presumptively

must have been a clean bookmaker in this case, else they would not have continued, and a reliable one, else over all these years they would not have essentially licensed him to run a bookmaking operation in this city. He turned out to be a quote 'embarrassment' for the Houston Police Department.''

The very idea that Bob would conspire with his brother to murder his wife was also absurd, Ramsey suggested.

''Are you going to pick somebody that's been blackmailing you over the years, are you going to pick somebody like that, who's as crazy as Roger Angleton is . . . ?

''Roger Angleton was a blackmailer, an extortionist. When he ran out of extortion money, he came back for one more dip.''

Ramsey reviewed some of Roger's stranger antics, and suggested that the evidence showed that Roger had been stalking Doris for most of the first part of the year. He read from some of Roger's writings, including the ''Elements of letters'' note found in the briefcase.

''Take it back and look at it,'' Ramsey urged the jury, ''and see what kind of scribbling this madman is doing in whatever—whatever his machinations were. He was a man descending into madness. He was on pills. He was obsessed by weapons. He had binoculars. He had aliases. He had the Hell Fire contraption [a device to make a semi-automatic weapon fire almost automatically]. He had the stinger [exploding] bullets. He had these rambling notes. He had stalking notes. He had Doris' license plates.''

Having sufficiently built Roger into a maniacal killer, Ramsey turned to his accomplice—the second shooter.

"There are two cars. There are two guns. The physical evidence from the medical examiner, the ballistics expert, and our reconstruction expert . . . all of them are consistent with only one thing, and that is that there were two people in that house.

"And why is that important? Because the three times a young white male, the last time one day before the shooting, at Budget Rent a Car, a young, athletic, slender white male, was identified as being with Roger Angleton during all these movements about the city. That's the second voice on tape . . . and for all we can tell during this trial, the police have never and are not now looking for that man."

Ramsey turned to the issue of the softball bat.

"The biggest red herring in this whole case is that Doris was sent back for a bat. Every mother at every game, all the proof shows, would take the children, drop them off, go back home, and then come back after practice was over and the game was in progress."

Doris had said she was going home to change clothes, Ramsey said; it was merely a coincidence that she'd been asked to bring the bat back with her.

"And this has turned into a living urban legend, this baseball bat mystery. It's a red herring. It teaches how little evidence the state has in this case."

As for the fingerprints on the money wrapper, Ramsey suggested that the wrapper came from Bob's safe after Roger had rifled it to get the money Bob had in it, the $10,000 or $12,000 Bob said had been stolen.

Of all the papers in the case, this was the only time any fingerprints were identified, Ramsey said.

"Now think about that," Ramsey said. "All the papers, all the places where Roger stayed, all the cars that he drove, there's no contact. There's no phone records. There's no nothing, of any contact between Roger Angleton and Bob Angleton but for that, those two fingerprints.

"The 'one-shooter' theory just doesn't make sense. What happened is, Doris walked into a situation where somebody was downstairs and somebody was upstairs. Whoever was upstairs came running down and she got caught between two people and they panicked and they shot her thirteen times. That's a panic situation. That's not some professional hit."

Bob had been completely cooperative with the police throughout, Ramsey said.

"All right. The HPD is in a situation where they're somewhat embarrassed because a problem informant, that is, somebody they allowed to work so that they can get information from him, is involved. They truly want the theories to fit. There was a divorce in progress. There was a lot of money involved. Therefore he must be guilty. He's the husband in a divorce and there's a lot of money.

"Well, so they tend, subconsciously, perhaps, but they tend to want to clear a case, and they clear a case because they fall into a tape recording made by this crazy man, that doesn't contain Bob's voice, but they want it to fit so they force it to fit. That amounts to willful blindness.

"Well, it's almost over. We're at the end. Remember, the verdict has got to be a unanimous verdict of each individual person. But we're at the end of a tragic affair now. When justice is done, the state always wins. Remember that. The state doesn't lose when you bring in a not-guilty verdict. You bring it in because that's what your conscience tells you to do.

"And now we're at the end of that tragedy. God bless Doris. May God wreak his justice on Roger. The fate of Niki and Ali and Bob now is in your hands. I think you will take care of it. Godspeed. There's a lot of evidence to look at. Take a look at it. Write a verdict of not guilty in this case.

"Remember, whatever the state says, ask what Ramsey would say."

Now it was time for Wilson and McClellan to step up and try to reclaim their momentum.

THIRTY-FIVE

Wilson started for the state.

There were five points, Wilson said, apart from the tape, that showed the guilt of Bob Angleton.

One was Bob's reaction to Roger's first demand for money back in 1991.

"All that was over Roger Angleton telling Bob Angleton that if he didn't pay him money, bad things were going to happen to his family, that he was going to the Internal Revenue Service and he was going to turn him in as a bookmaker.

"Now, the police already knew he was a book-maker . . . so was that a threat? No.

"So that leaves two other things. One is a threat to his family, to his children and his wife, and the other is a concern on his part about the IRS. Now, if you believed somebody was posing a threat to your wife and to your children, are you going to go to some lawyer and try to settle it over money? Or are you going to go to the police department to protect your family?

"What's he do? His money meant more to him than his family. His money and his concern about having to pay the IRS trumped any concern he had about those two kids and his wife, and he settled this thing for money, so that his brother wouldn't go to the IRS. That's what kind of husband and father this defendant is. Think about that."

While the defense might try to contend that Doris' divorce action was in abeyance, the facts showed otherwise, Wilson argued. The fact that almost $1.5 million had been found almost a year after Doris had first frozen the boxes, money that Doris hadn't known about, showed that Bob was holding out on Doris.

"Those records," Wilson said, "show that the day before Doris Angleton was murdered, Bob Angleton was in that box. Interesting timing.

"What was in that box but money? That may account for those fingerprints, which we will talk about in just a minute. But you see, when Doris filed for divorce, all of a sudden Bob Angleton is losing a lot.

He's losing a beautiful wife. The custody of the children obviously are going to be some sort of issue here that would be a concern to any father.

"I would guess he's losing the house in River Oaks . . . I don't think he made the payments on that with his little delivery service. But he's losing the River Oaks house.

"But you know, I think the big thing for Bob Angleton was the money. Because once again, now, that's the big issue. Bob's got lots of money. And we know he's got some tax problems probably as well. And we know that on April tenth, Doris went to Eddie Urquhart, who's a tax lawyer.

"So once again, just like back in 1991, what's the issue here? Taxes. See, when it gets down to his money and his taxes, family is second, money is first."

Wilson tried to put some life back into the "red herring," as Ramsey had referred to it, the softball bat. Wilson suggested that after Ali's practice in the batting cage, Bob went directly to his Blazer, but not before purposefully leaving the bat on the deck.

"Why would he leave the bat if he's going straight to his vehicle to leave, and he's in charge of the equipment? Why would he leave the bat by the back door, walk off from it, get in his truck and take off to go to the other field?

"Why? Listen to the tape of Bob and Roger. They've got to get her to the back of the house. We know from the testimony even of the daughters that Mrs. Angleton routinely would go home during batting practice. Well, she went home to change, she'd go upstairs. That's not where they wanted her to go. You heard that on the tape. How are you going to get her to the back door of the house? With the bat being back there.''

Wilson pointed out that Bob went to the game first to set things up.

''What's the first thing he says when he gets there? He unloads the bats, realizes [he] left Ali's bat back at the house by the back door. The two girls are at the house. They're going to be there for another hour. They are going to eat. They're going to do their homework. They're going to change, come to the game.

''Mom is there. Doris is there. She's feeding the kids. They're all going to come together. They've got phones in the house. He's sitting there with a phone in his pocket for an hour and a half and doesn't call, doesn't call his wife and say, why don't you grab the bat and bring it with you when you come down here?

''No. He waits until she gets all the way down there and turns around and sends her back. Try that with *your* wife some time.

''No. You know why? Tell you why. Because he has to get her separated from those girls and get her back to the house, to the back portion of the house. That's why he doesn't call her, because he has to make sure she went back to get the bat.''

Bob's actions at the Ella Lee house after the game were likewise peculiar, Wilson suggested.

''They get into the vehicle when the game is over, after an hour and a half of trying to get hold of her, drive home, drive up, drive next to the door, see the door is partially open. Before the girls can say anything, old Bob's got it in reverse and backing out.

"What threat could there possibly still be in that house? I mean, whatever happened to her, rationally thinking people would have believed that if there was some threat there, the threat is gone. My God, she hasn't answered the telephone or a page. She's been gone an hour and a half. You drive up, her car's at the front door. You've got to believe she's inside.

"No, there's not a man on planet Earth who wouldn't go in and check on his wife, just like that. And to make you think that he believed something bad could happen to him by not—that's insane. But hey, maybe on the old gumption scale he's not very high."

After reminding the jury that Bob had been told to enter the house by the police dispatcher, and that he even had Tex Welsh for backup, Wilson asked the question, "Why didn't you go in, Bob Angleton? You won't go in because you don't want to take a look at what you caused to happen to Doris. That's why he didn't go in."

Wilson suggested that the jury listen to the interview taped by Detective Wright.

"You listen," he said, "and tell me whether a man who thirty minutes earlier found out his wife had died, you tell me whether you spot any emotion on that tape at all, folks. I will bet you he had more emotion in his voice when he put out the football line on Saturdays and people called to bet, than he did when he talked to Mike Wright. He could have cared less."

And did Bob ever mention Roger's threats to Wright? Wilson asked.

"He never mentions Roger's name once to Mike Wright. He never mentions this note once. The first time this note comes in is the next day. And where is that? Over at George Tyson's office. And who does he give it to? A homicide detective? No. He gives it to Kevin Templeton.

"Why did he wait that long? Roger had to get out of town. See, it was always planned that Roger was going to be the guy, but the fact is, Roger hoped to be one step ahead of everything, and he had to give Roger time to get out of town. And that's why he never said anything about that."

Ramsey had referred to the absence of evidence of money going from Bob to Roger. Wilson wanted to deal with that.

"The last thing I want to talk to you about," Wilson said, "is the money in Las Vegas. Remember the testimony about the $64,000 Roger had? And remember the testimony about the money wrappers? See, the money wrappers were not wrapped around the money when they were found, were they? The money wrappers were in an envelope, separate from the money . . .

"And on one of the money wrappers . . . are two fingerprints of the defendant. And they want you to believe that maybe [it] was just a money wrapper, I guess, old Rog had kept around from this 1991 or 1992 settlement, just kept it in an envelope, I guess, as a souvenir.

"That money came out of that box on April fifteenth. You know that. We all know that. He took that money out on April fifteenth and gave it to Roger, so Roger could do what he wanted done . . . to have his wife murdered . . . so Roger would have money to get out of town and get started.''

But Bob had miscalculated, Wilson said. Bob never thought that Roger would ''surreptitiously tape him. And secondly, he never thought his fingerprints would ever be found. He figured Roger would get rid of all that.

''You know,'' Wilson said, ''just like what's on the tape, the first thing Roger says to Bob is this: Today's the day. Well, it is, today *is* the day. Today is the day that this man is held accountable for the tragedy that he caused to occur. He took Doris Angleton from all of us. He put those two little daughters where they will never see their mother again. All over money. Today is the day. It's time he paid.''

THIRTY-SIX

Now it was McClellan's turn, and McClellan hoped to spike the defense case once and for all, beginning with the ''two-shooter'' theory.

''Ladies and gentlemen of the jury,'' McClellan said, ''there is no two-gunman theory. There wouldn't make any difference in this case, whether there was a whole platoon [who] went into . . . Ella Lee. But the reason it's important to them is, because they have to explain the tape.

''For, if it's not Bob Angleton on that tape, who

is it? If it's not Bob Angleton on that tape, who is it? So, *they* say, it's a second gunman.''

McClellan scored off Ramsey's characterization of Doris' friends as ''the Briar Club ladies, Nancy Drew division.

''Heaven forbid that if you have a loved one, a friend, an associate, who is murdered and you dare talk to any of your friends about that situation. Be ready to be ridiculed, if the case ever comes to trial, because you're just—especially if you're women— you're 'gossipy.' ''

Doris' friends weren't gossiping, McClellan said, they were concerned about the future of the twins, who were the friends of their own children. They had no motive, McClellan said, to come into court and falsely say it was Bob on the tape.

''You know better than that,'' McClellan said. ''You know the worst, hardest thing for them to do was to be up there, saying, 'That's Bob Angleton. . . .' Just like several of them said, 'I was hoping it wasn't going to be [him].' ''

But it wasn't only Doris' friends who'd said it was Bob's voice on the tape, McClellan reminded the jury.

''You have Kevin Templeton. Kevin Templeton, who was reluctant, you could tell on the witness stand, to be up there testifying against Bob Angleton . . . who would know better than Kevin Templeton, dealing with him day in and day out, as to whose voice that was?''

The defense had its experts, McClellan said, but, ''I would suggest to you that you don't need an expert to determine the voice on that tape.

"If you-all were to listen to final arguments today, with your eyes closed, would there be any doubt at your ability to identify who the speaker was? If your eyes had been closed during the argument, do you think you could have picked out Mike Ramsey? Do you think you could have picked out Ted Wilson? Do you you think you could have picked out Lyn McClellan?"

The experts' tests had a built-in problem, McClellan said, in that only the exemplar could be used to compare Bob's voice to the voice on the tape. The jurors could listen to all the tapes, including the exemplar, and decide for themselves which sample of Bob's voice sounded most like the tape with Roger, the exemplar or one of the other samples.

The best example of Bob's true voice, McClellan said, was to be found on the FBI tape, because it was made when Bob didn't know he was being recorded. People talk differently when they're having conversation than they do when they're being interviewed, McClellan said.

The experts never interviewed Bob himself, McClellan pointed out; they had no way of knowing whether the exemplar was truly representative of the way Bob usually talked.

But all the exemplars and spectrographs in the world, McClellan now suggested, didn't amount to anything when measured against the meaning of the actual words spoken on the tape.

"I will suggest to you that [from] the content of the tape, you will know them by the words they speak. Listen to what they say and [you will] be able to identify who is saying what.

"Now . . . the defense's argument is that this was a frame-up, that this was a tape created by Roger. It's a discussion between Roger and the other, 'second gunman.' I suggest to you that's absurd. Because if that was a tape between Roger and the 'second gunman' going over this planned assassination, would there be any reason to have it *secretly* made? Would there be any reason not to have a good quality of tape?

"Would there be any reason not to refer—if you are going to frame Bob—[not to] say 'Bob' on the tape? You won't hear his name at all. You hear Roger's name several times, but you won't hear Bob's.

"There's no attempt there to frame Bob Angleton," McClellan continued. "There's not one thing that you can ever point to that [suggests] that Roger tried to frame Bob Angleton. The tape was accidentally discovered when he was arrested on some unrelated charge, in Las Vegas."

The idea that the tape was part of a frame-up just didn't hold up to scrutiny, McClellan said.

"I guess they would have you believe that Roger Angleton hired someone, created a script, and then had someone sit down and create a taped conversation, where that person was supposed to sound like Bob Angleton."

All the jury had to do to dismiss that notion, McClellan said, was simply listen to the tape.

"Just by listening to the tape, you can tell that's

not what occurred. That is not someone reading a script. They're talking over each other, and you can tell by the words that are said. You will know by the words who they are.''

The tape was of Bob Angleton instructing Roger on how to kill Doris, McClellan said.

There was almost no discussion between the voices about what each would do, McClellan added; if it were really a discussion between two gunmen, there would be evidence of planning of two, cooperative courses of action, not just one.

''There's no discussion about, 'Well, I'm going to go in this side and you will be, position yourself over there.'

''There's nothing like that. The reason there's not is because there's not two gunmen. There has to be two gunmen for Bob Angleton to get out of this, because otherwise that's his voice on the tape.''

A telling remark on the tape, McClellan said, came when Voice Number Two objected to the severing of a finger to get a ring.

''Why would a gunman worry about that?'' McClellan asked. ''A second gunman, he wouldn't care what you did. A person who is getting ready to [shoot someone] thirteen times, seven times in the head, cutting off a finger is going to be a problem?''

The context of all the remarks made by Voice Number Two indicated that it was Bob's voice on the tape.

''[They] talk in there about letting a dog out. Now, [why] would another gunman worry about letting a dog out, or not putting the dog out? If this is Roger

Angleton and a hired gunman, I know what you'd do with the dog. Number fourteen, boom. But not if you're the homeowner. Not if your kids love that dog. You don't hurt that dog. You've got to put it in its little cage.''

Virtually all of the exchanges on the tape, McClellan argued, showed that the discussion was Bob Angleton telling his brother what to do.

And despite Ramsey's argument that there was no evidence of remuneration, there was indeed such evidence, McClellan said, even on the tape.

''There's a contract for sure,'' he said. ''They talk on the tape, 'I don't get paid if I don't finish the job.' One person talking. [It's] not 'we' don't get paid if 'we' don't finish the job. *I* don't get paid if *I* don't finish the job.''

The very fact that the the two voices talked about the target's likely movements when she arrived home was significant, McClellan said. Roger Angleton wouldn't know that sort of information, and neither would the mythical second gunman.

Now McClellan moved into his peroration.

''I guess it's just a coincidence that only two months after Doris filed for divorce that this murder occurred. I guess it's just a coincidence that in fact Roger then appeared at that particular time, two months after the divorce [was filed], to kill Doris Angleton, that would have then saved him [Bob] having to split half his assets with her, that it's just a coincidence that it would also prevent the exposure of millions of dollars to potential tax liability.

''I guess it's just a coincidence that $64,000 in

cash is found on Roger in the briefcase. It's just a coincidence that that amount of money was there.

"I guess it's just a coincidence that the bank wrappers have Robert's fingerprints on them. I guess it's just a coincidence that on April 15, 1997, Bob went to the Citizens National Bank where $1.4 million was later found.

"I guess it's just a coincidence that on the night Doris was killed there was a softball game to assure that Bob and the girls would be one place and Doris would be another.

"I guess it's just a coincidence on that particular night that she had to be sent back to get a bat . . .

"I guess it's a coincidence that when Officer Carr came out and told Bob Angleton, 'Your wife is dead,' that he challenged him.

" 'How do you know she's dead? You are not a medical expert. You need to get someone over here to make sure she's dead.' Not somebody over here to make sure she's alive, because if she's alive, we've got a lot of problems. I need to know she's dead."

Now McClellan read from Doris' letter to Bob, the one written on February 7, in which she expressed fear over the "volatility" of the relationship.

" 'I'm sure you have some ideas, and have been thinking along these lines for some time. Love, Doris,' " McClellan concluded the letter.

"Bob had some ideas," McClellan said. "He's been thinking along certain lines for a certain time.

"I suggest to you that Bob had some ideas of what ought to happen. It's not anything that Doris knew about, and that idea was to solve this divorce real quick. No liability for taxes, no splitting of assets, and removing a person who was already going to be removed.

"Now they would have you believe that Roger Angleton just happened to pop up in Houston, Texas, on this particular day, and in a vengeful mood, just happened to accomplish all those things that would have been beneficial to Robert Angleton.

"The tape is right," McClellan said. "Today *is* the day. Today is the day that you get the case. . . . We now have to give it up and turn it over to you, but I have complete confidence in your ability to take care of that case, and to reach a rightful solution. Mr. Ramsey is right, the state wins when justice is done. And that's what we seek, justice in this case."

VERDICT

THIRTY-SEVEN

McClellan had had his moment of doubt in the days before the trial, in the aftermath of the Cain debacle. But during the heat of the trial, his optimism had returned.

Now that the jury had the case, McClellan felt even more confident. He believed that his arguments about the significance of the tape's content outweighed the voice charts of the two experts.

Bob's side was also confident; on the Friday before the closing arguments, the defense decided not to ask the jury to consider any possible lesser offense in its deliberations.

"We want to go for broke," Ramsey told the *Chronicle*'s Steve Brewer.

After McClellan's closing remarks, the case was delivered to the jury about 11:00 A.M. on Monday morning. Now Bob Angleton's life was in the hands of seven men and five women, who would have to evaluate the meaning of nearly 300 exhibits and the testimony of more than fifty witnesses.

The first day's deliberations ended with no verdict, and the judge ordered the jury sequestered in a downtown hotel.

The following day, however, the jury foreman sent notes to the judge reporting that they were at an impasse and that there was "no hope" of reaching a verdict. In one note, the foreman reported that the split was 10–2; in another, the split was 11–1.

McClellan and Wilson now considered whether to ask Rains to declare a mistrial, which would give them a chance to try the case over, with perhaps a quite different strategy on voice identification witnesses. Ramsey objected, and the judge agreed, saying it was too soon.

McClellan and Wilson thought the lopsided votes, with only one or two dissenters, was a good sign for the prosecution; generally such a split meant that there were one or two people holding out for an acquittal.

Tyson turned to McClellan after the 10–2 note came back.

"How do you think it's split?" Tyson asked.

McClellan shrugged, but was thinking that it was obvious that Bob's life was now hanging on just two votes. But getting over this last hurdle might be difficult.

"This is the type of case, you could probably convince somebody that there's reasonable doubt," McClellan said later.

Then, when the 11–1 note came back, McClellan began thinking he was going to have to retry the case, that the lone holdout would tie up the rest of the jury until the judge would be forced to declare a mistrial.

Tyson and Ramsey, meanwhile, seemed quite unworried, even when the vote moved from 10–2 to 11–1.

"They seemed to be very, very confident that this deal was going their way," McClellan said. "And I could never understand why. Then we went from 10–2 to 11–1. And they were even more confident it was moving their way. And I think any attorney worth their salt would be worried shitless that it was moving away from them."

After the judge instructed the jury to keep on deliberating, the panel was again sequestered for the night.

On Wednesday, as Bob and the lawyers filed back into the courtroom for the third day of deliberations, Ramsey came in smiling.

"Today's the day," Ramsey said, grinning.

"He was happy as all get-out," McClellan said later.

Ramsey's words, an obvious reference to the words on the disputed tape, sparked the first doubt in McClellan's mind that things might not be going as expected.

One of the reasons for the defense optimism, Stan Schneider said later, was that the sound of Cain's video deposition could be heard coming from inside the jury room on Tuesday. It was obvious that the jury was replaying the voice expert's testimony. If they were re-examining that crucial evidence after hours of deliberation, that probably meant they were getting close to reaching a verdict.

Then, after eighteen hours of deliberation, the jury sent one more note to the judge.

They had reached a verdict, they said.

*   *   *

By now the courtroom was jammed, while other on-lookers milled around outside, as one of Houston's most notorious murder cases appeared to be coming to a climax.

Have you reached a verdict? Rains asked.

We have, Your Honor, said jury foreman Johnnie Davis.

Not guilty.

As the words were read, Bob leaped from his chair and embraced Schneider and Tyson, tears flowing. McClellan and Wilson sat slumped in their seats. They had lost, and the worst of it was, they had done it to themselves.

THIRTY-EIGHT

How had something that looked like a slam dunk when the police had first found the casette recording that seemed so obviously proof of Bob and Roger plotting together come down to an acquittal?

After the verdict, the lawyers for both sides interviewed the jurors to find out how they had reached their decision. The key evidence, both sides learned, was Cain's videotaped deposition—evidence that wouldn't have existed had Wilson not thought it necessary to hire the expert.

Almost from the beginning, the last holdout told McClellan, four members of the panel were adamant for acquittal. That meant that the 10–2 and 11–1 votes had to be for Bob's innocence, not guilt.

The *Chronicle*'s Stefanie Asin caught up with two jurors, Sharon Mantzel and Johnnie Davis. Both said that while they weren't convinced that Bob was innocent, there was reasonable doubt about his guilt.

The jurors spent most of the time discussing the disputed tape, they said; opinions were split as to whether Voice Number Two was Bob's.

"I thought it sounded like Robert Angleton, and others didn't think it necessarily sounded like him," Mantzel said. But in the end there wasn't enough proof to say beyond a reasonable doubt that it was Bob, she said, particularly with the testimony of Cain.

The jury listened to both the disputed Brothers Tape and Cain's deposition over and over again, and in the end, concluded that there simply wasn't enough evidence to establish that the voice was Bob's.

"It comes to a point where you have to trust an expert," Mantzel told Asin.

That was the main point of the prosecution's second-guessing of itself as well.

"I guess what I wish I had done," McClellan said later, "was attack any voice identification expert. And show that you can't bring in—it's really analogous to a psychiatrist's testimony, someone who has never met a person, but who's trying to relate to something that happened a year before. How they were acting.

"Here's a person who comes in, who's never met the person whose voice it is, who's now trying to tell you, by him giving you an example, which is obviously going to be a self-given example, knowing that he's, if he gives it and you tie me to it, I'm dead, and he's going to say, yeah, that's the guy.''

After Cain's report came in, McClellan said, the
prosecution hired yet another voice expert to evaluate
the tape; this expert concluded that the voice *was*
Bob's. Meanwhile, the defense had a third expert
who said it wasn't.

''So we're gonna put a guy on, in rebuttal to say,
No it *is* Bob; then they'll come along right behind us
with their guy, who says, No it's not Bob. And then
the defense, if I'm the defense, what I'm going to
argue is, experts in the area—they've relied upon experts, we've relied upon experts, and the experts, they
cannot agree. If they can't agree, how can there be
anything but reasonable doubt in this case?

''So I'd just rather have—the first thing I did is
check with the FBI, and asked them to tell us what
the deal is, on voice identification. They sent us ar-
ticles that said lay-witness identification—ordinary
people—is more reliable than anything else in
existence. I should've just taken that and run with it,
and attacked all their experts. Because to me, their
presentation did not translate well in the courtroom.

''What I think the jury did was say, Well, he's a
scientist, and he worked for the Secret Service and
he worked for the IRS, and it's probably just like
fingerprints, even though it's not, and hasn't even
been admitted in court in the majority of the states.
That's where we lost the case, the experts.''

The whole science of voice identification, Mc-
Clellan said, was really more of an art; what the pros-

ecution should have done was attack the meaning of any of it.

The difficulty with that, however, was the fact that it was the state that brought Cain into the case to start with. It would have been much better for the prosecution if they had let Bob's side bring the expert on, and then attack the reliability and relevance of the science. Perhaps they might then have even been able to keep the whole subject away from the jury, as the defense had planned to do in the beginning, before Cain's devastating report.

And there were some who had still other ideas on why the jury had done what it had done.

One was Tom Conner, Doris' divorce lawyer.

Conner wasn't surprised at all by the verdict.

"I think when you put the two fourteen-year-old girls on the witness stand, I think it would be difficult for any jury not to think . . . now, am I going to make these girls orphans? So when people asked me my prediction about the murder trial even before it got started, I predicted that he would get a not-guilty. I mean, I just thought it was a terribly difficult case for the state.

"It was a great move to put those girls on the stand, [just after] their birthday, a year after their dad was arrested on their birthday. I mean, the girls' mom is dead, and now they're asking us to convict their daddy in a death penalty case?"

The jury's sentiment all along was with Bob, Conner thought.

THIRTY-NINE

So Bob the bookmaker was a free man; and for a man who calculated the odds so well and always had himself covered, if he had hired his brother Roger to kill his wife and had gotten away with it, he had made an enormous gamble and won.

True, there were costs that Bob would have to pay even if he was, in the eyes of the law, completely innocent. For one, there was all the notoriety, not something a quiet bookmaker likes to have; worse, by now everyone in Houston knew that Bob was not only a bookmaker, but a snitch as well.

There was a cost, in terms of exposure to the IRS; even while the trial was underway, Julie Hughes, acting as Bob's trustee, had paid about $1.5 million to the IRS as a good faith effort to resolve any lingering tax issues.

There was a further cost in terms of a rupture within his family. Doris' mother, Ann, at first thought Bob might have been involved, and then decided that he couldn't have been, it was unthinkable. Not so Steve McGown, her son and Doris' brother. Steve attended Bob's trial, and was convinced that Bob was responsible for Doris' death. He tried to get his parents to return the $1.6 million that Bob had divided with Doris, that Doris had put into the safe-deposit boxes she had rented in her and her parents' names. Steve was repulsed by the money; it was ''blood money,'' he told Ann. But Ann thought the girls might need it if Bob was convicted. Randy McGown gave the money back; the whole matter had left strains among everyone concerned.

And there was the opprobrium Bob's illicit activity had brought on the Houston Police Department, as Conner aptly summarized.

"From what I heard through this case, really makes you wonder," Conner said. "I know the police have to rely on informants, but if what I've read is correct, I mean, in essense the vice squad made Bob Angleton the most successful bookie in Houston, in the fourth largest city in the country. To me that's kind of like, if you've got organized crime, you leave the big fish alone and you keep getting little fish. It doesn't make sense."

That was a sentiment echoed by the *Houston Chronicle,* too, in an editorial a few days after Bob's acquittal.

"The strange case did not begin with the death of Doris Angleton, but years earlier when the Houston Police Department began to use Robert Angleton as an informant, at the same time tolerating his illegal gambling operation . . .

"American juries may or may not be more skeptical of the prosecution and more credulous of the defense than they used to be. However, the Angleton case should leave the Houston Police Department one lesson wiser: There is no good reason for turning a blind eye to an informant's wrongdoing. The consequences of doing so can be tragic and extreme. Had police acted more responsibly toward Angleton years ago, events might have taken a more benign course."

But the state of Texas wasn't entirely done with Bob; there was still the matter of all the seized money. They might not have been able to convict Bob for Doris' murder, but they could sure make him pay for his bookmaking.

A series of hearings was scheduled for the fall, in which the state attempted to get legal authorization to keep the $3.4 million it had seized. To get the money back, Bob would have to prove he was entitled to it.

To that end, Ramsey already began laying the foundations for a rather amazing, if shrewd claim: Bob Angleton earned that money as an informant for the police department. It was, in effect, Bob's payment for services rendered.

"I think we have a fairly strong position there," Ramsey told the *Chronicle*'s Brewer ten days after the acquittal. "I certainly wouldn't be reluctant to litigate that position because everything he did was done with the knowledge, consent, and sometimes advice of the authorities."

And finally, there was the matter of the $64,000 seized from Roger during his arrest in Las Vegas. Whose money was that? It couldn't be Bob's, of course, since Bob was acquitted of having given it to Roger for Doris' murder. Nevertheless, the state said it should keep the money because it consisted of proceeds from illegal gambling—Bob's gambling, not Roger's.

Not so, said Mark Bennett, Roger's old lawyer. That money belonged to Jennifer Manning, Roger's wife at the time it was seized.

"They just don't want anyone connected with Roger to win anything," Bennett said.

Doris was dead, Roger was dead, and Bob was exposed, as was the Houston Police Department; the Harris County district attorney's office was flummoxed by their own attempt to be clever.

Most of all, life would never be the same for Ali and Niki; those idyllic days on Ella Lee Lane were gone, fallen into the void left by Doris when she was taken in some sort of craziness that no one could ever truly understand.

Was Bob the victim, or was he the perpetrator?

Just like the Briar Club ladies, you could argue it either way; all bets were covered.

SHE LOVED HER SONS...TO DEATH.

Hush Little Babies

THE TRUE STORY OF A MOTHER WHO MURDERED HER CHILDREN

DON DAVIS

Not since the Susan Smith case has a murder so shocked the nation: a beautiful, loving mother is horrified to find her two young sons stabbed to death on her living room floor by an intruder. Hearts go out to poor Darlie Routier, who appeared to live for her children. But overwhelming evidence soon finds Darlie, the neighborhood's "Most Wonderful Mom," guilty of slaying her own innocent children in cold blood...